# 校区分布

**咨询电话：** 010-82611818
**工作时间：** 周一至周日 09:00-18:00

## 海淀区

魏公村中心　　水清木华中心　　总部南楼中心　　总部北楼

## 朝阳区

望京华彩中心　　建外SOHO中心　　国贸瑞赛中心

## 东城区

崇文门中心

## 顺义区

顺义祥云小镇中心　　欧陆广场中心

# 择校咨询

为了满足走国际路线家庭的多样化需求，新东方国际教育培训中心特别成立择校咨询团队，定期开展择校相关活动。

**国际教育线下展**：依托新东方集团的行业影响力，结合国际教育发展趋势，整合北京地区多元化教育资源，汇集北京地区国际部/校资深教育专家。为走国际路线的人群全力提供参与实体展会的机会，全方位展示各个学校的优质教育理念和资源，与其进行现场面对面交流。

**择校讲座/咨询**：择校专家均为北京新东方全职教师，拥有丰富的一线教学经验；同时深耕北京地区国际路线规划，将多年累积的国际视野、留学趋势、择校经验提供给新一代中国家庭。择校咨询服务专门针对北京地区提供公立学校国际部/国际学校的历史、课程设置、师资、升学情况、招生动态等全方面的基础信息介绍；为不同家庭提供择校咨询与留学备考长线规划。

**直播探校**：与校方合作开展深度探校活动，全程提供在线讲解、答疑，以第一视角带领家长步入校园，亲身感受学校氛围。

**家长社群**：100+ 定向社群，覆盖 6000+ 北京地区走国际路线的家庭；独享社群内部资料、一手信息、校方资源。

# 课程产品

| 课程 | 适用人群 |
| --- | --- |
| 托福 TOEFL | 小学~在职 |
| 雅思 IELTS | 初中~在职 |
| 小托福 TOEFL Junior | 小学~初中 |
| AP | 高中 |
| IB | 高中 |
| SSAT | 初中 |
| SAT | 高中~本科 |
| ACT | 高中~本科 |
| A-Level | 初中~高中 |
| GRE | 本科~在职 |
| GMAT | 本科~在职 |
| NCUK 国际预科 | 高中~本科 |
| OSSD 国际高中课程 | 初中~高中 |
| 精英计划 | 初中~在职 |

扫码关注视频号
了解更多精彩内容

# 新东方国际教育培训中心介绍

新东方国际教育培训中心（New Oriental Global Education Training）于 2020 年 11 月正式成立，由新东方教育科技集团旗下最核心的业务——新东方留学考试板块进行组织升级而来，脱胎于 1993 年创立的北京新东方国外考试部。

为更好地适应时代的变化和教育发展趋势，更好地服务国际教育领域的学生和家长，新东方国际教育培训中心的业务覆盖从低龄人群、中学人群、大学人群到成人人群的全年龄段国际教育培训领域。

课程产品包括留学考试备考辅导、国际学校备考辅导、国际学科（AP、A-Level、IB 等）、国际竞赛辅导、国际预科以及提升国际竞争力的各类英语能力和学科学术能力提升的课程和服务。旨在服务有国际教育需求的全年龄段客户，为其提供全学习链产品，帮助他们开拓全球视野、塑造独立人格、探究终身学习、履行社会责任，成为合格的世界公民。

新东方托福名师团力作

落笔生花

# 新托福学术写作
## 高分范文精选

TOEFL
Academic
Writing

史 禹  刘仁谦  薛 航  赵丹阳  蒙 欢
王元元  薛 白  杨丰璐  刘静灏  王 嘉    著

机械工业出版社
CHINA MACHINE PRESS

本书是一本全面指导新 TOEFL 考试学术写作（Academic Writing）模块如何进行撰写的书籍，也是市面上第一本同类参考书籍。

第一部分，详细介绍新 TOEFL 考试改革后的样式，特别是学术写作部分改革后的样式，并附有学术写作新的评分标准。第二部分，是新 TOEFL 学术写作高分范文，通过 20 道学术写作题，详细解读学术写作的出题点、构思、行文逻辑、论述步骤、词汇使用。每道写作题提供了至少两篇高分范文，题目和范文均提供中文译文。值得一提的是，这 20 道学术写作题均改写自 2020~2023 年独立写作真题（原考试题型），相应的范文都是由曾经被 ETS 评为满分的考场作文改编的。第三部分，是新 TOEFL 学术写作话题范文，更多话题，更多思路，更多视角，更多参考。

全书共有 67 篇范文，助力你备考新 TOEFL。先模仿，再超越，不断思考，自我精进，这样距离梦想的 TOEFL 分数会越来越近。

## 图书在版编目（CIP）数据

落笔生花：新托福学术写作高分范文精选／史禺等著. —北京：机械工业出版社，2023.6（2024.10 重印）
ISBN 978-7-111-73419-2

Ⅰ.①落… Ⅱ.①史… Ⅲ.①TOEFL-写作-自学参考资料 Ⅳ.①H315

中国国家版本馆 CIP 数据核字（2023）第 110527 号

机械工业出版社（北京市百万庄大街 22 号 邮政编码 100037）
策划编辑：苏筛琴　　　责任编辑：苏筛琴　张若男
责任校对：孙铁军　　　责任印制：单爱军
保定市中画美凯印刷有限公司印刷
2024 年 10 月第 1 版第 6 次印刷
184mm×260mm・16 印张・1 插页・328 千字
标准书号：ISBN 978-7-111-73419-2
定价：68.00 元

电话服务　　　　　　　　　　网络服务
客服电话：010-88361066　　　机　工　官　网：www.cmpbook.com
　　　　　010-88379833　　　机　工　官　博：weibo.com/cmp1952
　　　　　010-68326294　　　金　书　网：www.golden-book.com
封底无防伪标均为盗版　　　　机工教育服务网：www.cmpedu.com

# 推荐序

1993 年，新东方从面向大学生的 TOEFL、GRE 语言与考试培训起家，至今已经走过整整 30 个春夏秋冬。30 年间，千万学子以新东方为共同的母校，将梦想带向世界，将美好带回中国。30 年间，新东方国际教育见证了 TOEFL 考试一次又一次的改革，新东方国际教育的各业务单元，围绕考试培训进行一次又一次贴近考试本身、贴近客户需求的深耕，帮助一届又一届的考生，迈过 TOEFL 考试的坎，走向属于自己的更高平台。

2023 年，伴随着 TOEFL 考试的新一轮改革，新东方国际教育北京学校的研发部门，精心编写了这本《落笔生花——新托福学术写作高分范文精选》，立足市场需求，着眼考生关切。这是市场上第一本围绕改革后 TOEFL 学术写作题型撰写方法论的参考资料，由新东方国际教育多名高分数、高年资、高评价名师合力执笔，由内部研发中心负责审阅、校对，完全经得住考场实战的检验，不枉负学员和家长口碑的信任。这本书，在相关同类素材匮乏的档口，对为了实现梦想而挥洒汗水的考生，能起到指路明灯的作用。希望这抹光亮，可以帮助迷茫中的考生找到方向，提拾信心。但愿这抹书香，可以助力挣扎中的考生补足力量，抵达辉煌。

耿耿

新东方国际教育北京学校总经理

# 序言

2023年3月25日，一个平静的周六傍晚，我在微信朋友圈刷到了一个不平静的消息：某外网平台爆料，ETS官方将于2023年4月12日对外召开发布会，正式宣告TOEFL考试将于2023年7月26日改革。

我将信将疑，但还是更偏向于相信。因为这个爆料者在2019年春天，也做了类似的预告，随即被2019年8月1日起的TOEFL瘦身改革实锤印证。

2023年4月8日，我参加了新东方国际教育北京学校的春季择校展，有幸被安排到展会的ETS展台，协助ETS的工作人员，对前来咨询ETS旗下考试信息的家长进行答疑。

毫无疑问，很多家长在那个敏感的时间点，都在求证TOEFL改革消息的准确性。我当然也顺便问了一下和我同一个展台的ETS工作人员，这改革的消息是真的吗？对方没有确认，也没有否认。

也是在那个展会上，我收到了一张ETS China某位老师赠送的，4月12日下午在北京瑰丽酒店进行的"2023年托福考试全新升级发布会"的邀请函。我这才反应过来，原来这个发布会还有现场版，真是满满的仪式感。

4月12日，我去了那个现场发布会，感受到了气氛，收获了真相：改革是真的，不用怀疑了。

这里面有个大家不知道的情况，从2020年3月底ETS开始推出TOEFL在家考以来，我和我的工作团队，因为工作原因，需要频繁接触这个在家考，给需要考试的学生提供考务细节咨询。2021年，我们萌生了一个想法：组织学校内部有实力考到TOEFL写作单项30分的老师去参加考试，考后立即回忆出自己的独立写作文章，然后静等ETS打分。如果几天后出的分数真的是30分，那么对应的文章我们就收集起来，目的是为了整理成一本书。以当时的视角看，市面上的 TOEFL 写作书很多，多一本、少一本不那么有所谓。**但我们认为我们的这本书会很有亮点，因为它是被 ETS 评为满分的范文，而不是"我认为是满分"的作文。**

事实上，在 2023 年 3 月初，我们这本准备出版的书，已经完成了版权协议签署、排版、校对等环节。如果没有 TOEFL 改革的消息，这本书会在 2023 年 5 月份问世。

但 TOEFL 改革的消息打乱了我们原有的安排，也"废掉了"市面上现有的几乎所有针对 TOEFL 独立写作的范文参考资料。我看着出版社发来的排好版的精美 PDF，有诸多不舍。转念一想，在这个改革的档口，围绕改革后 Academic Writing 的素材十分有限，题目少、范文少、点评也少，对于那些明确在 2023 年 7 月 26 日之后才要考试的学生来讲，备考材料太过单薄。如果我们把原本要出版的独立写作范文集，改写成改革后 Academic Writing 的样子，毫无疑问会给考生们在迷雾中指明一些方向，于是我开始重新组织老师们进行文章的改写工作。

TOEFL 改革后，新增了 Academic Writing，而取消了原来的独立写作。词数从原来的 300 个起，变为改革后的 100 个起。本质上，ETS 只需要考核原来 1/3 篇幅的内容就可以判定一个考生的写作水平，但从新的评分标准来看，对语言的能力要求没有本质改变。结合 ETS 官方提供的少量 Academic Writing 的样题，我们对 20 篇来自考场内还原的满分或近满分的独立写作范文进行了改写，力求贴近改革后学术写作的样子。读者朋友们在阅读时会发现，Part 2 每个新托福 Academic Writing 题目的范文后面，都有一份成绩单截图。这些 Academic Writing 的范文，就是根据对应作者回忆当次满分或近满分的独立写作（改版前）文章的改写。改写过程中，不少参与者都花费了不少精力，一度也很焦虑，怎么改都觉得还可以更好。并且我们邀请这 20 篇文章的作者，互相点评他人的文章，告诉读者，这文章好在哪里，还有哪些美中不足。此外，我们还为文章提供了核心词摘录和参考译文，希望读者可以从中找到仿写、创作的灵感，有朝一日到考场上也能收获属于自己的新写作 30 分。

在本书的重新编写过程中，除了对应文章的原作者之外，我们团队中的张超群、乔明睿也给予了支持，对稿件进行审阅，在这里表示感谢。张超群在北京新东方长期从事模考批改工作，见证了近年来几次围绕 TOEFL 考试的大大小小的改革。乔明睿也从事模考批改工作，入职新东方的时间不长，在 2023 年 4 月 8 日参加了一次 TOEFL Essentials（TE）考试，写作单项取得满分（12 分），所以我们放心让她做一部分改写工作。了解 TE 这个考试的考生们都知道，改革后的 TOEFL Academic Writing，就是 TE 写作单项的一种题型。

本书几经校稿，也难免有疏漏之处，欢迎各位读者批评指正。

最后，我想花些篇幅介绍一下本书的几位原作者，是他们的综合脑力智慧，促成了这本书的问世。

史禹，曾任新东方国际教育北京学校副校长，从事教学工作 16 年，先后参加过 20 次 TOEFL 考试，1 次获得口语满分，多次获得写作单项满分。

赵丹阳，TOEFL 写作、AP 微观经济学教师。托福 111 分（阅读、写作满分），雅思 8.5 分，持有国家高中英语教学资格证书以及国际认证非英语国家英语教学能力 TKT 证书（M1-M3 满分）。

刘仁谦，TOEFL 写作教师，香港理工大学同声传译硕士，托福 115 分，写作单项多次满分。出版过的书籍包括《一本书改掉托福写作顽疾》《一本书扫清 SAT 语法盲点》。

蒙欢，美国哥伦比亚大学硕士，加拿大多伦多大学本科。托福 116 分，阅读、写作双满分。擅长培养学生的逻辑思考能力与美式思维能力。

王元元，北京外国语大学英语语言文学专业硕士研究生。持有 CATTI 英语二级笔译证书、英语专业八级证书、高中英语教师资格证书、TKT 证书。托福 111 分，写作单项满分。

薛白，北京外国语大学硕士研究生、威斯康星大学麦迪逊分校教育学院访问学者。英语专业八级，托福 112 分。教授写作多年，托福写作多次考取满分。

薛航，国际教育培训圈资深写作教师，在参加过的托福考试中，写作单项多次获得满分。除了托福写作之外，对 GRE/GMAT 写作也有深入了解。

杨丰璐，完成收录至本书中的那篇改写的托福写作满分范文的时候，是一名高三年级（12年级）的学生，后来被英国 UCL 大学录取，前途无量。

刘静灏，业内资深 TOEFL 口语教师，高中曾就读于北京某知名国际学校，本科毕业于美国西雅图华盛顿大学。虽然是名口语教师，但写作也经常考到 30 分。

王嘉

新东方国际教育北京学校教学研发负责人

# 目录

推荐序

序 言

## Part 1　新版托福考试知多少？

01　新版托福考试简介 ……………………………………………… 002
02　新版托福学术写作简介 ………………………………………… 005

## Part 2　新版托福学术写作高分范文

Topic 1　购物的选择问题 …………………………………………… 012
Topic 2　老师是否应该布置每日作业？ …………………………… 018
Topic 3　教育的目标应该是什么？ ………………………………… 024
Topic 4　现代人给宠物花的钱太多了吗？ ………………………… 030
Topic 5　现在比过去更容易接受教育吗？ ………………………… 036
Topic 6　招商引资 or 保护环境，哪个更优先？ ………………… 044
Topic 7　在国内 or 出国研学旅行？ ……………………………… 050
Topic 8　自主阅读比老师留的阅读作业重要？ …………………… 056
Topic 9　分任务完成 or 一起完成小组作业？ …………………… 062
Topic 10　分任务完成 or 一起完成小组作业？ ………………… 068
Topic 11　该不该限制大学涨学费？ ……………………………… 074
Topic 12　年轻时出国旅游更好 or 老了以后出国旅游更好？ … 082

| Topic 13 | 该不该期望别人保持礼貌? | 088 |
| Topic 14 | 暑假上课 or 参观博物馆? | 094 |
| Topic 15 | 放任朋友犯错比伤害友情好? | 100 |
| Topic 16 | 儿童进行小组活动比独自活动好? | 106 |
| Topic 17 | 面对问题应该轻松 or 严肃? | 112 |
| Topic 18 | 政府花钱探索太空是不是浪费钱? | 118 |
| Topic 19 | 追随本心 or 遵守传统社会规则? | 124 |
| Topic 20 | 教师收入是否应该和学生的成绩挂钩? | 130 |

## Part 3  新版托福学术写作话题范文

▶ 教 育 类 ............................................................................ 137
| Topic 1 | 老师要不要每天留作业? | 138 |
| Topic 2 | 自己帮同学 or 建议同学问老师? | 142 |
| Topic 3 | 高中教师最重要的能力是什么? | 146 |
| Topic 4 | 培训重点教师 or 所有教师各自上网课 | 150 |

▶ 生 活 类 ............................................................................ 155
| Topic 5 | 政府建设大型设施要求人们搬迁对不对? | 156 |
| Topic 6 | 改善健康靠控制饮食 or 适量锻炼 or 缓解压力? | 160 |
| Topic 7 | 学生交朋友最好的方式是什么? | 164 |
| Topic 8 | 没有理由不讲礼貌? | 168 |
| Topic 9 | 年轻人是否缺乏独立性? | 172 |
| Topic 10 | 父母要不要每周给孩子零花钱? | 176 |
| Topic 11 | 经济条件不同的人能不能做朋友? | 180 |

▶ 社 会 类 ............................................................................ 185
| Topic 12 | 有钱就应该做慈善? | 186 |

| Topic 13 | 要不要为了保护环境减缓经济发展？ | 190 |
| Topic 14 | 新能源 or 传统能源，哪个更好？ | 194 |
| Topic 15 | 在市中心划定无车区 | 198 |
| Topic 16 | 谦虚 or 展示自我，哪个更重要？ | 202 |
| Topic 17 | 谁最需要政府补贴？ | 206 |

## ▶▶ 工作类 ......... 211

| Topic 18 | 想要商业成功必须打广告？ | 212 |
| Topic 19 | 不能接受批评的人在团队中是不会成功的 | 216 |
| Topic 20 | 找工作的途径 | 220 |
| Topic 21 | 节假日不收发工作邮件能否提高员工的满意度？ | 224 |
| Topic 22 | 好队友最重要的品质是什么？ | 228 |

## ▶▶ 政府类 ......... 233

| Topic 23 | 建新房 or 保护历史建筑？ | 234 |
| Topic 24 | 为吸引游客，政府要不要改善治安和市貌？ | 238 |
| Topic 25 | 投资实物 or 投资环境美化？ | 242 |

# Part 1
# 新版托福考试知多少?

众所周知,新 TOEFL 考试将于 2023 年 7 月 26 日改革。改革之后,新版托福考试阅读模块仅考查 2 篇文章;听力模块考查 2 个对话和 3 篇演讲;口语模块仍保持原来的 4 个任务;写作模块删除原有的独立写作,保留综合写作,新增学术写作。

## 01 ➤ 新版托福考试简介

新版 TOEFL 考试，于 2023 年 7 月 26 日起在全球落地，这是 ETS 对 TOEFL 考试做的一次重要改革。

新版 TOEFL 考试全程仅需要约两个小时，阅读将仅考查两篇文章，不再有不算分的加试题目存在，也将取消原有的独立写作题目，加入 discussion board（讨论板）形式的新写作题目。

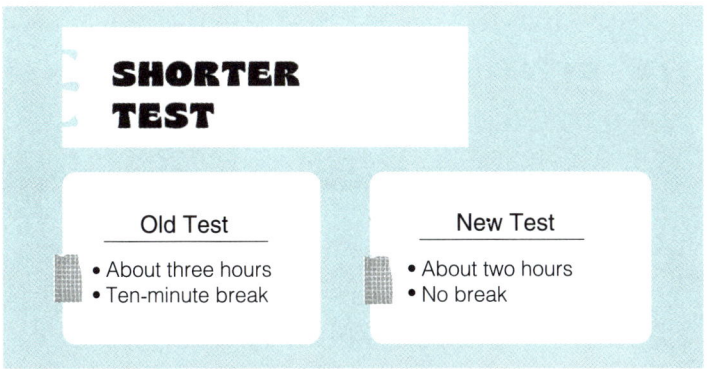

新版 TOEFL 考试，全程用时约 2 小时，将比现行 IELTS、PTE 等标准化考试用时都要短。改革之后，每一个线下考试日都将安排上午场和下午场两场可选的 TOEFL 考试，ETS 此举是为了给考生提供更多的选择、更好的考试体验。

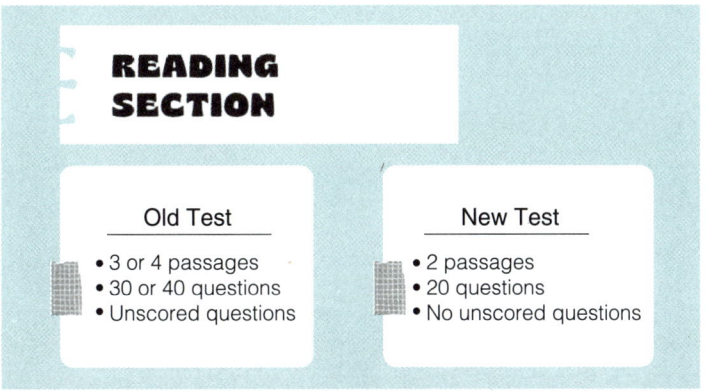

新版 TOEFL 考试，具体到阅读单项，将从原来的一次考查 3~4 篇文章、30~40 道题的形式，压缩到只考查 2 篇文章、20 道题，总时长 36 分钟。改革前可能存在的阅读加试，将不复存在。

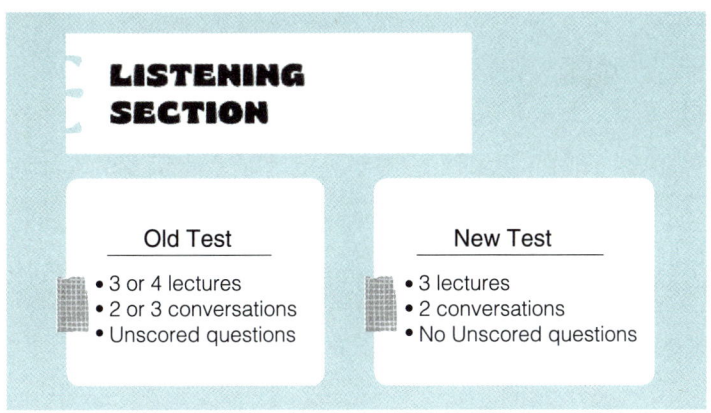

新版 TOEFL 考试听力单项，将从原来的单次考试 3~4 个 Lecture，2~3 个 Conversation，压缩到仅存在 3 个 Lecture、2 个 Conversation，总计 28 道题的模式，同样也不存在听力加试。

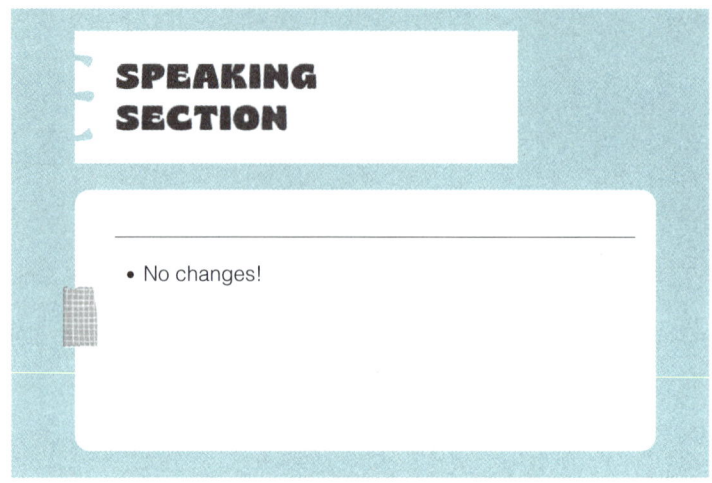

新版 TOEFL 考试，在口语环节没有变化，还是 4 个 Task。

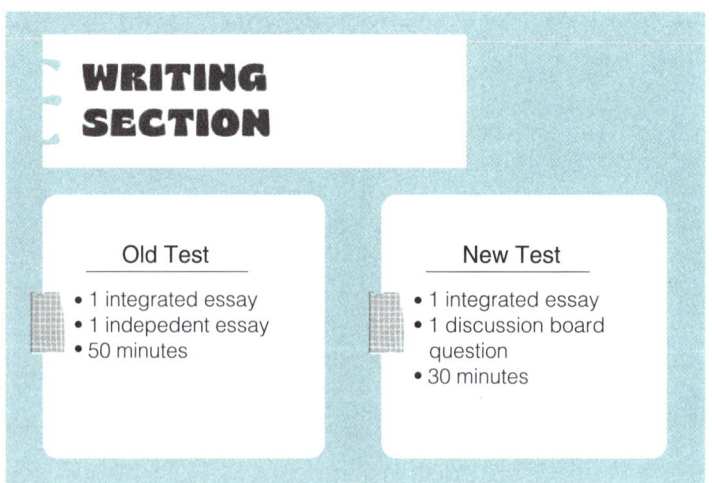

新版 TOEFL 考试，变动最大的就是写作部分。原有的综合写作部分依然保留，标准作答时间仍然是 20 分钟；但独立写作部分取消了，变成 discussion board（讨论板）形式的写作，取名叫 Academic Writing（学术写作），且这部分用时仅 10 分钟。因此，新版 TOEFL 写作环节，考试时间将从原来的约 50 分钟，压缩到约 30 分钟。

## 02 ▶ 新版托福学术写作简介

备注：样题来源于托福考试官网。

新版 TOEFL 考试写作部分的 discussion board 环节，样题参照上图。教授围绕一个话题引发讨论（在图中，样题话题有关政治科学），该话题可能与政治、经济、文化、教育、体育、科技等相关（样题话题讨论发展经济和保护环境哪一个更重要）。教授先提供一段背景信息，围绕这些背景信息，抛出讨论的话题。两名学生后续围绕这个特定话题开展讨论。

需要考生在 10 分钟的时间内，读完屏幕上的阅读材料，理解并提取陈述双方的立场，思考他们观点的优势与不足之处，在之后自己的作答当中，补充自己的看法，并且要求在现有两个人观点的基础上，有新的看法。需要考生们注意的是，10 分钟作答时间是包括阅读材料时间在内的，因此实际键盘敲入学术写作作答的时间是不足 10 分钟的，并且作答需要至少 100 词。这对于学生多方面的能力提出了新的挑战，比如阅读理解能力、快速提取信息的能力、思维组织能力、打字速度跟上思维进度的能力，等等。

Susan: I would prioritize the environment. We only have one planet and if we don't take care of it, we won't have pleasant lives in the future. Economic growth can be important, but not at the expense of the environment. I think we need to shift towards more environmentally-friendly economic practices, such as investing in renewable energy and promoting environmentally-friendly technologies. We'll all live much healthier lives if the world around us is clean.

Alex: While I agree with Susan that environmental sustainability is important, I think that economic growth is the only way to solve many of the social and economic problems we face. We need a strong economy to create jobs, reduce poverty, and improve standards of living. Not only that, but if companies grow stronger and more profitable, they might eventually develop new technologies that solve our environmental problems.

I strongly agree with Susan's idea that our lives will be unpleasant if we focus entirely on economic growth. I would add that if the environment is damaged by industrial development we'll be more likely to suffer from ailments like cancer and lung disease. Alex raised the relevant point that we can count on profitable companies to solve problems using new technology, but he didn't mention that they might arrive far too late to be of use. For example, it could take decades for an innovative company to create a clean energy source, but people are affected by environmental catastrophes right now. Overall, then, I'd say that companies and governments should prioritize the environment at this time.

上图左部是两个学生 Susan 和 Alex 在围绕教授抛出的话题展开自己的讨论。

Susan 认为保护环境更重要，否则我们未来的生活将不会美好。经济发展固然也很重要，但我们需要发展的是对环境友好的经济，比如投资可再生能源、促进对环境友好的技术的发展。总之，Susan 想表达的观点就是"绿水青山就是金山银山"。

而 Alex 认为，Susan 的观点固然有一定道理，但发展经济才能解决现实中的很多问题。一个坚实的经济基础，可以帮助创造诸多工作岗位、减少贫困、提升人们的生活质量。只有一个企业的经济实力提升了，有了足够的利润，才能有实力发展新科技，去解决我们遇到的环境问题。总之，Alex 的观点就是"经济发展是第一生产力"。

上图右部是围绕样题话题作答的范文。考生先强调同意 Susan 的观点，即不能把所有的关注度都放在经济增长上面。( I strongly agree with Susan's idea that our lives will be unpleasant if we focus entirely on economic growth. )

随后，考生需要补充自己的观点，因此有了 I would add that 之后的内容。考生提到，如果环境因经济发展被破坏了，我们会有可能患癌和肺部疾病。( I would add that if the environment is damaged by industrial development we'll be more likely to suffer from ailments like cancer and lung disease. )

再之后，考生也指出了 Alex 观点的不足，并举例进行论证。考生提到，如果等那些有实力的企业研发出既能发展经济，又足够环保的新技术，恐怕真等不及。因为一个新兴企业可能需要十几年才能研发出新能源，但是人们当前正被恶化的环境深深影响着。（Alex raised the relevant point that we can count on profitable companies to solve problems using new technology, but he didn't mention that they might arrive far too late to be of use. For example, it could take decades for an innovative company to create a clean energy source, but people are affected by environmental catastrophes right now. ）

论述的最后，考生总结陈述了自己的观点，使得讨论的内容前后自洽、有始有终。（Overall, then, I'd say that companies and governments should prioritize the environment at this time. ）

- I strongly agree with [student]'s idea that [mention one point made by the student].
- I'd add that [elaborate on the point with your own idea].
- [The other student] raised the relevant point that [mention one point made by the other student], but he/she didn't mention that [challenge that point].
- For example [elaborate on your challenge with your own ideas].
- Overall, then, I'd say that [directly answer the question].

I strongly agree with Susan's idea that our lives will be unpleasant if we focus entirely on economic growth. I would add that if the environment is damaged by industrial development we'll be more likely to suffer from ailments like cancer and lung disease. Alex raised the relevant point that we can count on profitable companies to solve problems using new technology, but he didn't mention that they might arrive far too late to be of use. For example, it could take decades for an innovative company to create a clean energy source, but people are affected by environmental catastrophes right now. Overall, then, I'd say that companies and governments should prioritize the environment at this time.

上图左部，是围绕样题话题作答过程中，考生采用的行文框架，即学生们喜欢的"模板"。但我们不鼓励大家在真实作答中套用模板，还是要结合具体需要讨论的话题，就事论事，不生拉硬套。作答的关键是要贡献自己的观点，是否一定要引用、评论其他人的观点，视情况而定。

新版 TOEFL 考试的综合写作部分，还是采用原有的评分标准。但学术写作部分，适用新的评分标准，具体的英文、中文版评分标准参照如下。

# TOEFL iBT®
## Writing for an Academic Discussion Rubrics

| SCORE | DESCRIPTION |
|---|---|
| 5 | **A fully successful response**<br>The response is a relevant and very clearly expressed contribution to the online discussion, and it demonstrates consistent facility in the use of language.<br>A typical response displays the following:<br>• Relevant and well-elaborated explanations, exemplifications, and/or details<br>• Effective use of a variety of syntactic structures and precise, idiomatic word choice<br>• Almost no lexical or grammatical errors other than those expected from a competent writer writing under timed conditions (e.g., common typos or common misspellings or substitutions like there/their) |
| 4 | **A generally successful response**<br>The response is a relevant contribution to the online discussion, and facility in the use of language allows the writer's ideas to be easily understood.<br>A typical response displays the following:<br>• Relevant and adequately elaborated explanations, exemplifications, and/or details<br>• A variety of syntactic structures and appropriate word choice<br>• Few lexical or grammatical errors |
| 3 | **A partially successful response**<br>The response is a mostly relevant and mostly understandable contribution to the online discussion, and there is some faciltiy in the use of language.<br>A typical response displays the following:<br>• Elaboration in which part of an explanation, example, or detail may be missing, unclear, or irrelevant<br>• Some variety in syntactic structures and a range of vocabulary<br>• Some noticeable lexical and grammatical errors in sentence structure, word form, or use of idiomatic language |
| 2 | **A mostly unsuccessful response**<br>The response reflects an attempt to contribute to the online discussion, but limitations in the use of language may make ideas hard to follow.<br>A typical response displays the following:<br>• Ideas that may be poorly elaborated or only partially relevant<br>• A limited range of syntactic structures and vocabulary<br>• An accumulation of errors in sentence structure, word forms, or use |
| 1 | **An unsuccessful response**<br>The response reflects an ineffective attempt to contribute to the online discussion, and limitations in the use of language may prevent the expression of ideas.<br>A typical response may display the following:<br>• Words and phrases that indicate an attempt to address the task but with few or no coherent ideas<br>• Severely limited range of syntactic structures and vocabulary<br>• Serious and frequent errors in the use of language<br>• Minimal original language; any coherent language is mostly borrowed from the stimulus |
| 0 | The response is blank, rejects the topic, is not in English, is entirely copied from the prompt, is entirely unconnected to the prompt, or consists of arbitrary keystrokes. |

## TOEFL Academic Writing 评分标准
适用于2023年7月26日之后的新版TOEFL考试学术写作部分

| 分数 | 描述 |
|---|---|
| 5 | **是一份十分成功的作答**<br>作答内容与主题相关，表达清晰，对线上讨论做出意见贡献，语言运用表现出很出色的流畅性。<br>主要作答的表现为：<br>• 相关且详尽的解释、示例和/或细节；<br>• 有效使用各种句法结构，用词选择准确、地道；<br>• 几乎没有任何词汇或语法错误，除了那些可以预期到的有能力的作者在限时条件下出现的写作错误（例如，常见的拼写错误或像 there/their 这样的替换）。 |
| 4 | **是一份总体成功的作答**<br>作答内容与主题相关，且可以对线上讨论做出意见贡献，语言的流畅性使得作者的想法易于被理解。<br>主要作答的表现为：<br>• 提供了相关且充分阐述的解释、示例和/或细节；<br>• 输出了多种句法结构，选词恰当；<br>• 几乎没有词汇或语法错误。 |
| 3 | **是一份部分成功的作答**<br>作答主体和题目相关且易于理解，对线上讨论做出了意见贡献，在具体语言使用方面有一定程度的流畅性。<br>主要作答的表现为：<br>• 部分解释没有陈述清楚、一些必要的例子缺失、不清晰或不相关；<br>• 作者使用的语法结构和词汇存在一定程度的多样性；<br>• 作者存在一些易被发现的词汇和语法错误，如单词形式、词组的使用错误等。 |
| 2 | **是一份大部分不成功的作答**<br>作答尝试表述观点，努力对线上讨论的话题做出意见贡献，但语言运用的局限性使得作者的本意难以被理解。<br>主要作答的表现为：<br>• 作者没有详细阐述自己的想法，或陈述的观点仅部分和题目相关；<br>• 作者使用的语法结构和词汇较为有限；<br>• 作者存在较多句子结构使用错误或单词形式使用错误。 |
| 1 | **是一份不成功的作答**<br>作答不能有效地对线上讨论的话题做出意见贡献，语言运用的局限性阻止了作者意思的表达。<br>主要作答的表现为：<br>• 作者运用一些单词或词组，在努力尝试回应相关讨论，但几乎没有连贯的想法；<br>• 作者的作答所使用的词汇和语法结构有限；<br>• 作者的作答频繁出现一些很明显的语言使用错误；<br>• 作者的作答存在较少的目标语言或存在较多的借用语言，与话题本身关联性不大。 |
| 0 | 作者作答记录为空白，或与话题本身无关，或作答语言不是英语，或作答语言拷贝自前文提示，或只是随意敲击了几下键盘，无法形成自己的意见。 |

# Part 2
# 新版托福学术写作高分范文

评判一篇"范文"是否真的够"范",实践是检验真理的唯一标准。只有在实考中取得过满分或接近满分成绩的范文,才真正值得学习。

这部分的 42 篇范文均是由考场满分或接近满分的独立写作文章改编而来。Academic Writing 词数从原来 Independent Writing 的 300 个起,变为改革后的 100 个起。从新的评分标准来看,对语言能力的要求本质没有变。所以,我们本着求真的原则,结合 ETS 官方提供的少量 Academic Writing 样题对之前的满分范文进行了改写,力求贴近改革后 Academic Writing 的样子。

# Topic 1
## 购物的选择问题

Section 1 of 1

Your professor is teaching a class on advertising. Write a post responding to the professor's question.

**In your response, you should do the following.**
- Express and support your personal opinion.
- Make a contribution to the discussion in your own words.

An effective response will contain at least 100 words.

Professor

When making a major purchase, like buying a car or a computer, we are influenced by a lot of factors: recommendations from friends or colleagues, information from the media (for example, TV, newspapers, or magazines), recommendations from a salesperson in a store, some other factors, to name a few. Which factor would most influence your decision? Why?

00:09:59　　Hide Timer

Paul

I believe that advertisements play a significant role in influencing my shopping decisions. In today's society, we are exposed to numerous advertisements, whether we are browsing our phones, logging onto websites, or waiting for the bus. When an advertisement recommends a product that I find appealing and needed, there is a high chance that I will go ahead and purchase that product.

Kelly

The recommendations of salespeople can be a deciding factor in whether I choose to purchase a product or not. Salespeople interact with many customers daily, and they understand the preferences of different groups of people from a larger sample. Therefore, I believe that when they recommend specific products to me from the vast array of options, there must be a reason behind it.

## 审题 & 构思

购物选择的话题，本身也是选择的一种，实际撰写过程中可以有很多种立场，没有对错。本题的文字阅读部分，Paul 和 Kelly 已经分别围绕自己的观点提出了各自的简要观点，而我不同意他俩任何一个人的观点，于是构思另辟蹊径，这样发挥的空间更大。这道题我提供了两段参考范文，核心观点相同，都是要相信朋友的推荐，而不要相信媒体或销售人员的推销，具体论述的侧重点不同。第一个范本作答里，我提出朋友不会欺诈。第二个范本作答里，我提出事情的反面，广告或销售人员很可能带着目的在推销，暗含欺诈。供读者们参考。

## My answer 1

According to the discussion, I hold the opinion that recommendations from friends are most reliable,[1] which is different from Paul and Kelly's standpoints. Friends generally have no *incentive* to lie to you or *exaggerate* the desirable quality of the products.[2] Additionally, friends may well be the users of the products and thus have the *first hand experience*.[3] For instance, when I was deciding to buy a new car, I was torn between buying a traditional gas car or an electric car. I read a lot of information on the Internet and on the magazine. But all the information was in conflict, with some claiming the gas car has greater advantages like going over long distances and some claiming that electric cars are quieter and have more *horsepower*. In the end, I had to consult a friend who recently bought a Tesla car. And he told me electric cars are definitely better than gas cars because charge stations are everywhere and charge fees are significantly lower than gas prices. After hearing from his first-hand experiences, I made up my mind to buy an electric car.[4] (184 words)

[1] 主题句：朋友的推荐是可靠的。

[2] 解释主题句：朋友可靠的原因是因为朋友没有动机对商品进行宣传。

[3] 段内递进：朋友推荐可靠的第二个理由是他们可能有产品使用的一手经验。

[4] 看到这道题目我脑海里很快浮现出几个生活中虚假广告宣传的例子，于是决定确定我的立场为：买贵重物品应该选择将朋友的意见作为重要参考标准。我首先论述了朋友的意见为何可靠，因为朋友没有欺骗的动机，会给予真诚的意见。而且朋友会把最宝贵的使用体验告诉你，我买电动车就是基于朋友的使用体验。举例论证，用个人购买特斯拉汽车的例子论证了朋友推荐的好处。消费决策过程包括信息对比、心理纠结以及最终选择朋友的推荐，过程论述详细。

## My answer 2

The sources mentioned by Paul and Kelly all have their innate flaws.[5] We are living in a commercial era, with financial inventiveness underlying nearly every activity in our lives.[6] Information from media is mostly commercial advertisements to trump up the desirable qualities of the products without disclosing their downsides. An advisement for a cellphone may claim its battery can last up to 24 hours without stating the fact it is achieved with minimal application running and screen light.[7]

Salespersons are the same. It is common sense that all salespersons work on commissions, which means that the more they sell to you the more they can make. Considering this, how can we trust salespersons as a reliable source of information? A newspaper report is a case in point. A girl, in order to improve her appearance, buys 30,000 dollars' worth of face masks which purportedly are made from natural herbs in a remote Tibet village from a salesperson in a beauty salon. As it turns out all the masks are made from synthetic materials and even without the approval of drug administration and may cause harm to skin.[8] (187 words)

[5] 主题句：其他消费推荐方式各有内在缺陷。

[6] 背景论证：商品时代充满利益动机。

[7] 分类论证：用手机续航为例论证商业广告会隐瞒产品缺陷。

[8] 这道题目还有一种写法，我想从商家角度论述商家推销的目的是赚钱，所以会隐瞒负面信息，比如手机续航时间就是个夸大宣传。而且销售人员推销的目的是抽成，难免会造成虚假销售。我想到了最近看到的假天然面膜的广告，于是将此作为论证。
分类论证二：用消费者重金购买虚假宣传的面膜产品的新闻报道论证销售人员的推销不可靠，达到用事实报道论证的有力写作效果。

| Words & Phrases ||
|---|---|
| incentive 动机 | trump up 捏造 |
| exaggerate 夸大 | commission 佣金，回扣 |
| first hand experiences 第一手的经验 | beauty salon 美容院 |
| horsepower 马力 | synthetic materials 合成材料 |
| innate flaws 固有的缺陷 | the approval of drug administration 药监局的批准 |

> **参考译文**

Professor

在购买大件物品时,例如购买汽车或电脑,我们会受到很多因素的影响:举例来说,朋友或同事的推荐、媒体(例如电视、报纸或杂志)信息、来自店家销售人员的推荐,以及一些其他因素。哪个因素对你的决定影响最大?为什么?

Paul

我相信广告在影响我的购物决定方面发挥着重要作用。当今社会,无论是浏览手机时、登录网站时,还是等公交车时,我们都会接触到无数的广告。当广告向我推荐我觉得有吸引力和需要的产品时,我很有可能会选择购买该产品。

Kelly

销售人员的推荐可以成为我是否选择购买该产品的决定性因素。销售人员每天与许多客户打交道,他们可以从更大的样本中了解不同人群的喜好。因此,我相信当他们从浩如烟海的选择中向我推荐特定的产品时,一定有其背后的原因。

## ■ My answer 1

　　根据上面的讨论,我认为朋友的推荐是最可靠的,这和 Paul 以及 Kelly 的观点不同。朋友一般没有动机对你撒谎或夸大产品的质量。此外,朋友很可能是产品的使用者,因此有第一手的经验。例如,当我决定购买一辆新车时,我在购买传统汽油车还是电动车之间纠结。我在互联网和杂志上阅读了很多信息,但所有的信息都是冲突的。有些人声称汽油车有更大的优势,比如能长途驾驶,而有些人声称电动车更安静、马力更大。最后,我不得不咨询一位最近购买了特斯拉汽车的朋友。他告诉我,电动车肯定比汽油车好,因为充电站到处都是,而且充电费用明显低于汽油价格。聆听了他的亲身经历后,我下定决心买一辆电动汽车。

## My answer 2

　　Paul 和 Kelly 提到的信息来源都有其内在缺陷。我们生活在一个商业时代，生活中的每一项活动都离不开利益动机。媒体信息大多是商业广告，其目的是夸大产品的理想品质而不披露其缺点。一则手机广告可能声称电池可以续航 24 小时，但没有说明这是在最少应用程序运行和最暗屏幕下实现的。

　　销售人员也是如此。众所周知销售人员工作都是为了拿佣金，这意味着他们卖给你越多，他们就能赚得越多。考虑到这一点，我们怎么能相信推销人员是一个可靠的信息来源？一则新闻报道是一个好例子。一个女孩为了改善自己的外表，从美容院的销售人员那里购买了声称是由西藏偏远村庄的天然草药制成的价值 30000 美元的面膜。事实证明，所有的面膜都是由合成材料制成的，甚至没有获得药品管理部门的批准，而且可能会对皮肤造成伤害。

作　者：史禹

成绩单：

Your Scores from Test Date:
**September 27, 2021**

| Total<br>(0–120) | Reading<br>(0–30) | Listening<br>(0–30) | Speaking<br>(0–30) | Writing<br>(0–30) |
|---|---|---|---|---|
| 113 | 30 | 29 | 24 | 30 |

# Topic 2
# 老师是否应该布置每日作业？

Section 1 of 1

Your professor is teaching a class on pedagogy. Write a post responding to the professor's question.

**In your response, you should do the following.**
- Express and support your personal opinion.
- Make a contribution to the discussion in your own words.

An effective response will contain at least 100 words.

Professor

The topic of homework is often a contentious one. While some believe that daily assignments are essential for optimizing learning outcomes, others contend that it is sufficient for teachers to assign tasks without specifying a daily quota. For our next class, I invite you to reflect on the question of whether teachers should assign homework that students must do every day. Looking forward to hearing your thoughts.

00:09:59  Hide Timer

Julia

I think assigning homework every day has a number of benefits, particularly for those who are not quite self-disciplined or lack an effective learning habit. After all, the teacher has already helped them organize their daily tasks, such as which assignments should be completed on Monday, Friday, etc. This would clearly save students a significant amount of time that they would otherwise spend making study plans themselves.

Stephen

In my opinion, this strategy may produce counterproductive effects on cultivating a good learning habit. For example, my high school English teacher used to require us to learn twenty new words each day, a seemingly reasonable requirement, as almost every language teacher would agree upon the importance of daily accumulation. Unfortunately, if we failed to keep up with the daily requirement due to a more important matter or illness, we would fall behind. Then, catching up with the missed days would become difficult and the whole idea of learning new words daily would be trivialized and eventually abandoned.

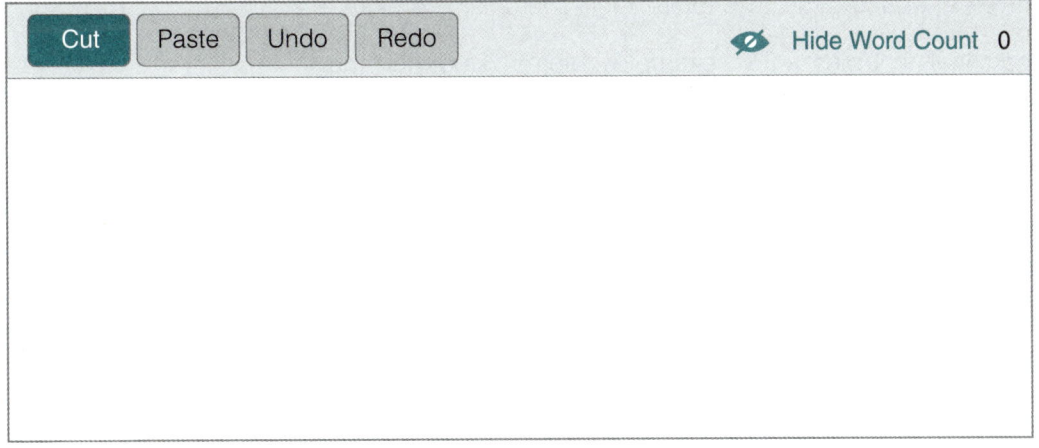

## 审题 & 构思

教授引导学生们进行讨论，老师是否应该每天都给学生布置作业。这是一道"应该"或"不应该"的题目，难度不算高。作者给出了两个版本的回答，第一个版本同意某一位同学的看法，同时进行理由上的补充。第二个版本采用了中立的写法，"是"与"否"取决于不同的情况以及不同的需求。由于考试时间以及段落篇幅的限制，段落展开的逻辑需要更加简洁清晰，同时举例论证也需要更加简短，更多采用"点到为止"的方式。

## My answer 1

I agree with Stephen that assigning everyday homework would bring about more negative effects than positive ones on students' learning.[1] In addition, I believe that the daily workload can impede students' opportunities for exploratory learning.[2] The vast preponderance of educators has more or less come to an agreement that learning should not be a one-way impartation of knowledge from teachers to students. Instead, students should be given adequate time to explore their interests and pursue personal hobbies. For example, some students may choose to volunteer at a community event, assist the elderly at a nursing home, or participate in a sports game or music festival outside of school.[3] Therefore, it is essential to provide students with enough space and time to pursue their passions beyond the classroom. (127 words)

[1] 明确表明自己的立场，同意 Stephen 的观点，认为每日作业弊大于利。

[2] 在 Stephen 看法的基础上进行补充，认为每日作业还会消极影响学生们的课外探索性学习。

[3] 用具体的例子展现了各种各样有意义的课外活动。

Topic 2　老师是否应该布置每日作业?

## My answer 2

I think whether or not daily homework is necessary depends on the individual student and the subject being taught.[4] Some subjects, such as math or foreign languages, require daily practice and repetition in order to fully grasp the material.[5] For these subjects, assigning daily homework can be helpful in reinforcing concepts and improving understanding. However, for other subjects that may require more creativity or critical thinking, such as literature or social studies, assigning daily homework may not be as effective.[6] It could lead to a focus on completing tasks rather than engaging with the material in a more meaningful way.[7] Thus, teachers should assign homework based on the course goals and the students' needs. (114 words)

[4] 采用了中立"it depends"的写法,提出具体情况具体分析。每日作业是否有效取决于不同的学科以及学生的需求。

[5] 对于一些需要日常积累的学科,比如数学和外语,每日作业确实有助于学生巩固所学知识。

[6] 对于一些需要发挥创造力或辩证思维的学科,如文学和社会学,就没有必要布置每日作业。

[7] 进一步提出了布置每日作业的弊端,会让学生们过分专注于完成作业,而不是寻求更有意义的方式参与学习和思考。

### Words & Phrases

| | |
| --- | --- |
| exploratory learning 探索式学习 | reinforce concepts 强化概念 |
| vast preponderance 优势比例 | course goals 课程目标 |
| a one-way impartation of knowledge from teachers to students 从老师到学生的单项知识传授 | |

参考译文

Professor

家庭作业的话题往往是一个有争议的话题。虽然有些人认为每日作业对于优化学习成果至关重要,但其他人则认为教师分配任务就足够了,而无须指定每日配额。下一节课,我请大家思考一下老师是否应该布置学生每天必须做的家庭作业的问题。希望看到大家的意见。

Julia

我认为每天布置家庭作业有很多好处,特别是对于那些不太自律或缺乏有效学习习惯的人。毕竟,老师已经帮他们安排好了日常任务,比如哪些作业应该在周一、周五完成等。这显然可以为学生节省大量的时间,否则他们可能会花更多时间在自己制订学习计划上。

Stephen

在我看来,这种策略可能会对培养良好的学习习惯产生适得其反的效果。例如,我的高中英语老师曾经要求我们每天学习 20 个新单词,这看起来是一个合理的要求,因为几乎所有的语言老师都会认同日常积累的重要性。不幸的是,如果我们由于更重要的事情或疾病而无法跟上日常的要求,我们就会落下积累任务。然后,想赶上那些落下的日子(的任务)将变得(更加)困难,于是每天学习新单词的整个想法将变得琐碎并最终被放弃。

## ■ Sample answer 1

　　我同意 Stephen 的观点,每天都布置作业会带来更多的负面影响。此外,这还可能阻碍学生探索学习的机会。绝大多数的教育工作者都或多或少地达成了一个共识:学习不应是教师向学生单向传授知识的过程。应该给学生足够的时间让他们自己去探索和发展个人兴趣爱好。例如,有些学生可能会选择在社区活动中做义工,帮助养老院的老人,或参加学校之外的体育比赛或音乐节。因此,为学生提供足够的空间和时间去参与他们感兴趣的活动是至关重要的。

## ■ Sample answer 2

　　我认为是否需要每天布置家庭作业取决于学生个体和所教授的科目。有些科目,如数学和外语,需要每天练习和重复才能完全掌握材料。对于这些科目,布置日常家庭作业有助于巩固概念和提高理解能力。但是,对于其他需要更多创造力或批判性思维的科目，例如文学或社会研究，每日家庭作业可能没有那么有效。这可能导致学生过度专注于完成任务，而不是以更有意义的方式去学习和理解。因此，教师应根据具体课程目标和学生需求来布置家庭作业。

作　者：赵丹阳

成绩单：

Your Scores from Test Date:
**May 19, 2021**

| Total<br>(0 – 120) | Reading<br>(0 – 30) | Listening<br>(0 – 30) | Speaking<br>(0 – 30) | Writing<br>(0 – 30) |
|---|---|---|---|---|
| 111 | 30 | 28 | 23 | 30 |

Your Scores from Test Date:
**April 18, 2023**

| Total<br>(0 – 120) | Reading<br>(0 – 30) | Listening<br>(0 – 30) | Speaking<br>(0 – 30) | Writing<br>(0 – 30) |
|---|---|---|---|---|
| 116 | 29 | 29 | 29 | 29 |

**MyBest™ Scores** as of April 27, 2023
Your highest section scores from all valid test dates are shown below.

| Sum of Highest Section Scores<br>(0 – 120) | Reading<br>(0 – 30) | Listening<br>(0 – 30) | Speaking<br>(0 – 30) | Writing<br>(0 – 30) |
|---|---|---|---|---|
| 118 | 30<br>Test Date: May 19, 2021 | 29<br>Test Date: Apr 18, 2023 | 29<br>Test Date: Apr 18, 2023 | 30<br>Test Date: May 19, 2021 |

# Topic 3
# 教育的目标应该是什么？

Section 1 of 1

Your professor is teaching a class on education. Write a post responding to the professor's question.

**In your response, you should do the following.**
- Express and support your personal opinion.
- Make a contribution to the discussion in your own words.

An effective response will contain at least 100 words.

Professor

Today we are going to talk about the goal of education. Educators are supposed to impart knowledge to students. On the other hand, it is a growingly popular idea that the most important goal of education today should be to teach people how to educate themselves. If you had to decide what the very goal of education is, what would you choose? Why?

00:09:59  Hide Timer

Lance

I would say the goal of education should be to teach people how to educate themselves. Unlike thirty years ago, when we did not have the ability to equip learners with the tools to learn by themselves, now the abundance of educational tools makes self-educating easy, efficient and economical. We have access to knowledge that used to be far beyond our reach in the past. This means that everyone that has access to Internet can have the most outstanding educational resources in the world. Self-educating has never been easier, and to teach people how to educate themselves is surely a necessity.

Parker

I cannot agree with Lance. We may assume that Internet is like the oxygen of the 21st century, but the sad truth is that still a large portion of the global population does not have an easy access to the online sensational world. This means that self-educating is still a luxury in many countries and regions. To make things worse, other media for self-educating, some traditional methods like public libraries and public schools, are facing tremendous challenge, which may come from a shrinking public budget or social riots. In a word, self-educating is still only a beautiful dream for a lot of unfortunate people, and is thus not the fundamental of education.

| Cut | Paste | Undo | Redo | | Hide Word Count 0 |

## 审题 & 构思

教育话题永远是托福考试最常见的话题，不管是改革前还是改革后。对于本题而言，在学生 A 和 B 已经给出双方的各自意见之后，我们能做的就是进一步为其中一方做补充，给出更多的、更细节的例证，以及更多的理由。对于教育目标这一话题，我在文章中继学生 B 之后进一步阐述了自学的局限性，并列举了教育需要做的具体事项，从而让讨论更完善，结论更全面。

Lance 开头提出自己的观点：教育应该教会学生怎么去教育自己。后面陈述理由，如今人们有更多途径进行自我教育，但怎么用好这些工具，其实是需要有人教的。后来又将当今互联网时代和 30 年之前有限的学习条件相比，论证网络学习资源的丰富性。

Parker 同样开头亮出自己的观点，后面的解释推翻了刚才 Lance 陈述的基础。Parker 的观点是：不能以偏概全，不是所有人都有机会上网；传统的图书馆、公立学校等学生可以接受教育的地方，现在也面临严峻的挑战，以此说明为什么靠网络进行自我教育不可行。

## My answer 1

The more important goal of education, by my account, is still the very nature of education: to pass the knowledge to the next generation, and to change their lives in a positive way.[1] Like what Parker said, self-education is not a **ubiquitous** character in the world, so we still need the traditional method: letting the schools and the teachers do their job.[2] To facilitate this process, there are lots of things that can be done and need to be done: we must[3] provide the teachers with better and more comprehensive training so that what they teach is always correct and up-to-date; we must provide the schools with better equipment, like microscopes and computers, so that students can feel the **essence** and happiness of learning in a more direct way;

[1] 作者认为更重要的教育目标是传播知识启迪下一代。

[2] 提出公立教师教育的重要性。

[3] 一口气连用四个 we must，罗列了自己的想法，用分号隔开，既显得有层次，又显得有气势。符合 5 分评分标准里的 "Relevant and well-elaborated explanations" "Effective use of a variety of syntactic structures and precise, idiomatic word choice" "Almost no lexical or grammatical errors" 的要求。

we must raise the salaries of teachers so that the current ones become more motivated, and the prospective ones are more attracted; we must urge the governments to prioritize education over things like religion, politics, and temporary economic growth. Only in this way can we ensure that our children have a bright future, and only in this way can we say that the most important goal of education is reached.[4] (199 words)

[4] 倒装句的应用，增加了句式的多样性，这是新标准里拿高分的一个点。

## My answer 2

I agree with Lance[5] in his perspective that to teach people how to educate themselves is the priority in the field of education. There will be a day when you stop learning from a teacher or professor, but it does not necessarily mean that you stop learning altogether.[6] In fact, sometimes it is the things that you learn by yourself after graduation that really matter. Without these things you teach yourself, you may find it difficult to compete in the labor market only with the knowledge you learned from teachers. A student majoring in computer science may learn C language and C++ in college, but he or she has to master Java and ASP. NET as well in order to work in companies like Google and Amazon.[7] Same logic also applies to students of other majors.[8] What is more, Internet is not the only means by which you can teach yourself useful knowledge. Books and magazines, for example, offer access to it as well. That is what Parker fails to see[9] when he argues that without Internet, self-education is nothing. (179 words)

[5] 提出了相反观点。

[6] 说理论述自学能力对一个人一生成长的重要性。关于这一点，我们每个人都感同身受。毕竟一个人在学校的时间总归是短暂的，学习本身又是不能停止的。这个时代也不允许我们停下学习的脚步。具体作答时，可以把这些意思表达出来，辅以例证，使得论述更加有层次，有力度。

[7] 例证。

[8] 推进论述道理的普遍性。

[9] 最后不忘再"踩"一脚Parker，使得论述的逻辑成完整的闭环，同意Lance，否定Parker，中间夹杂理由和事例。

| Words & Phrases | |
|---|---|
| abundance 大量 | essence 本质 |
| far beyond one's reach 遥不可及 | prospective 潜在的 |
| sensational 极好的；绝妙的 | prioritize 优先安排 |
| a shrinking public budget or social riots 缩减的公共预算或社会骚乱 | perspective 观点 |
| ubiquitous 十分普遍的 | priority 当务之急，首要事情 |

参考译文

Professor

今天我们要谈谈教育的目标，教育者应该向学生传授知识。另一方面，越来越流行的观点认为，当今教育最重要的目标应该是教会人们如何进行自我教育。如果需要你做一个决定，说明教育的真正目标是什么，你会怎么选择？为什么？

Lance

我想说教育的目标应该是教会人们如何进行自我教育。现在不同于30年前，当时我们没有能力为学习者配备自学工具；现在丰富的教育工具使自学变得简单、高效和经济。我们可以获得远远超出我们过去能力范围的知识。这意味着每个能上网的人都可以拥有世界上最优秀的教育资源。自我教育从未如此简单，因此教会人们如何自我教育无疑是必要的。

Parker

我不能同意Lance的观点。我们可能会认为互联网就像21世纪的氧气，但可悲的事实是，全球仍有很大一部分人无法轻松访问绝妙的网络世界。这意味着自学在很多国家和地区仍然是一种奢侈。更糟糕的是，其他用于自我教育的媒介——一些传统方法，如公共图书馆和公立学校，正面临着巨大的挑战，这可能来自缩减的公共预算或社会骚乱。总之，自学对于很多不幸的人来说仍然只是一个美好的幻想，这并不是教育的根本。

### My answer 1

在我看来，教育更重要的目标仍然是教育的本质：将知识传递给下一代，并以积极的方式改变他们的生活。就像Parker所说的那样，自我教育并不是世界上普遍存在的特征，所以我们仍然需要传统的方法：让学校和老师做好他们的工作。为了促进这一进程，有很多事情可以做，也需要做：我们必须为教师提供更好的、更全面的培训，使他们所教的内容始终是正确和最新的；我们必须为学校提供更好的设备，如显微镜和计算机，让学生能够更直接地感受到学习的本质和快乐；我们必须提高教师的工资，让现在的教师更有动力，让未来的教师更有吸引力；我们必须敦促各国政府将教育置于宗教、政治和临时经济增长之上；只有这样，我们才能确保我们的孩子有一个光明的未来；只有这样，才能说我们达到了教育的最重要目标。

## My answer 2

我同意 Lance 的观点，即教会人们如何进行自我教育是教育领域的首要任务。总有一天你会停止向老师或教授学习，但这并不一定意味着你完全停止学习。事实上，有时候真正重要的是你毕业后自己学到的东西。如果没有这些你自学的东西，你可能会发现仅凭从老师那里学到的知识很难在劳动力市场上取得竞争力。一个计算机专业的学生在大学里可能会学习 C 语言和 C++语言，但他或她必须同时掌握 Java 和 ASP. NET 才能在谷歌或亚马逊等公司工作。同样的逻辑也适用于其他专业的学生。更重要的是，互联网并不是一个人可以自学有用知识的唯一途径。例如，书籍和杂志也提供可以接触到这些知识的途径。Parker 认为如果没有互联网，自我教育便一无是处，这个观点是不妥的。

作　者：刘仁谦

成绩单：

Your Scores from Test Date:
**May 24, 2021**

| Total<br>(0–120) | Reading<br>(0–30) | Listening<br>(0–30) | Speaking<br>(0–30) | Writing<br>(0–30) |
|---|---|---|---|---|
| 114 | 29 | 29 | 26 | 30 |

# Topic 4
# 现代人给宠物花的钱太多了吗?

Section 1 of 1

Your professor is teaching a class on social science. Write a post responding to the professor's question.

**In your response, you should do the following.**
- Express and support your personal opinion.
- Make a contribution to the discussion in your own words.

An effective response will contain at least 100 words.

Professor

Our dogs and cats have always made us feel good about ourselves and we spend more on our pets these days than ever before. Before next class, I would like for you to discuss this question: Do people nowadays spend too much money on their pets (dogs, cats, or other animals)? Why do you think so?

00:09:59   Hide Timer

Smith

I think people nowadays spend too much money on their pets. It is estimated that pet spending exceeds 72 billion dollars every year, including food, vet care, pet services, supplies, etc. To be honest, I don't think spending 200 dollars on a dog's haircut is necessary, given that many poor families still need money to eat and live. Therefore, we need to budget for pet costs, and the money saved can be spent on better causes like charities and education. The sooner you cut expenses on pet care, the more options you will have to make a better life.

Zoe

Pets are part of our family. They give us love, pleasure, and companionship. It is noted that pet ownership can improve physical and mental health. Dog owners can have more exercises and cat owners experience less loneliness. They are priceless friends with few demands. When we spend time and money on pets, we want to make sure they are living a healthy and respectful life because we are the only supporters they have. Spending money on our pets can put a smile on our faces because we love to see pets are well fed and well cared for. It is the same way we see our loved ones being taken good care of.

| Cut | Paste | Undo | Redo | Hide Word Count 0 |

### 审题 & 构思

看到这道题目心中窃喜，宠物话题，相对好写，贴近生活，谁都不会无话可说。针对这道题目，不同人群可以有两种立场，也就是两种答案。对于确实在宠物消费上有铺张浪费现象的人群，可以谈需要理智消费，把省下来的钱用在更需要的地方，比如教育开支或者健康的社交活动。但是对于那些需要宠物陪伴来消除孤独感的人群，比如退休老人，适度的宠物消费可以让他们有满足感或者幸福感。所以，不同的限定条件会得出不同的结论，不要有绝对化的结论。

Smith 用每年美国宠物消费超过 720 亿美元的数据引出了过度消费的观点，并指出在宠物美容上过度消费的不合理性。还提出节约的开支可以用于慈善事业以帮助低收入人群，此观点有其合理性。

Zoe 从宠物对人类的情感满足这一点出发论证了宠物消费的合理性。因为宠物可以让人排解孤独，所以宠物消费越多，宠物越健康，人们心理满足感越强。但是 Zoe 忽略了过度消费的现象，这一点可以作为批驳的依据。

### My answer 1

I think Smith is making a good point because those who should be investing more wisely.[1] Take students for example. Their primary task is to obtain a satisfactory academic performance as well as gaining various skill sets that serve as the basis for a positive future development. Instead of allocating their allowances or savings from part-time jobs to pets, they should be purchasing books or attending training programs that would aid their comprehension of the class materials they learn at school.[2] In addition, it is also of great necessity for them to register for numerous extracurricular activities including sports teams or the debate club, where they are able to gain a diversity of essential skills such as cooperation, leadership,

[1] 摆明立场，同意 Smith 的观点，并直接指出过度消费的观点是针对消费不理智的人群。

[2] 作者用学生举例，提出学生应该把主要精力和金钱放在学业上，用 should 和 would 表示"学生应该做什么"这种高分虚拟语气句型论证教育开支的重要性。

and communication. All of these require a substantial financial investment.³ However, today, we often see students buying pet toys or foods using their pocket money. This is a strong indicator that they are spending more than necessary on pets since there are other more important aspects for them to invest in.⁴ (172 words)

③ 作者的第二个分论点：学生也有必要多多参与丰富的课外活动以获得重要的人际沟通技巧，这些也需要一定的消费，所以过度的宠物消费不合理。

④ 指出孩子如果把零花钱都花在宠物身上，会减少教育开支，这是得不偿失的。

## 📝 My answer 2

I agree with Zoe's opinion. I think money invested in caring for their pets is well-spent. Many elder retirees usually spend most of their days alone, and hence their pets act as the only true companion, friend, or even dependents of them.⁵ Take my neighbors as an example. They are a retired couple, and their children have grown up and formed their own families, so the old couple live on their own. Before they owned pets, their days were often dull and boring. But after they adopted two dogs and one cat, their lives have completely changed. By raising these small animals, the couple gradually began to realize their own worth and value. They felt that although they no longer had a job to attend, there are still animate creatures that are in need of their care. At the same time, the animals also provide the couple with unmitigated joy and love.⁶ Although the pets' daily expenditures amount to a large portion of their pension, the couple's investment is certainly worth the price, for they find the existence of the pets extremely healing.⁷ (183 words)

⑤ 作者指出宠物会给退休老人排解孤独，成为他们最好的陪伴，这是宠物消费合理性的心理原因解释。

⑥ 作者用退休邻居养宠物的例子论证了宠物对退休人员的重要性。对比了养宠物前无聊的生活和有了宠物之后充实有价值感的生活，从而证明了宠物对老年人的价值。

⑦ 作者指出老年人在宠物身上的消费是值得的，因为在照顾宠物过程中治愈了自己，升华了主题。

| Words & Phrases | |
|---|---|
| charity 慈善组织 | elder retirees 老年退休人员 |
| companionship 陪伴 | animate 有生命的 |
| gain a diversity of essential skills 获得多种基本技能 | in need of 有……的需要 |
| substantial financial investment 大量资金投资 | unmitigated joy and love 无与伦比的快乐和爱 |
| pocket money 零用钱 | the pets' daily expenditures amount to a large portion of their pension 宠物的日常开支占他们养老金的很大一部分 |

## 参考译文

Professor

我们的宠物，比如小猫、小狗，总是能让我们开心，我们和宠物相处的时间也越来越长。下节课前，我希望你们能讨论下这个问题：人们今天是否在宠物（猫、狗或者其他动物）方面消费过多？

Smith

我认为现在的人在宠物身上花了太多的钱。据估计，每年的宠物消费超过720亿美元，包括食品、兽医护理、宠物服务、宠物用品等。说实话，我不认为花200美元给狗理发是必要的，因为许多贫困家庭仍然需要钱来吃饭和生活。因此，我们需要对宠物费用进行预算，省下的钱可以用在更好的事上，如慈善机构和教育。你越早削减照顾宠物的开支，你就会有更多的选择来使生活变得更好。

Zoe

宠物是我们家庭的一部分。它们给我们带来爱、快乐和陪伴。据悉，饲养宠物可以让身体和精神都更健康。养狗的人可以进行更多的运动，养猫的人可以减少孤独感。它们是无价的朋友，要求很少。当我们在宠物身上花费时间和金钱时，我们要确保它们过着健康和受尊重的生活，因为我们是它们唯一的支持者。在宠物身上花钱可以让我们脸上有笑容，因为我们喜欢看到宠物吃得好，被照顾得好。这与我们看到我们的亲人得到良好照顾的方式是一样的。

■ My answer 1

我认为Smith说得很有道理，因为有些人确实应该进行更明智的投资。以学生为例。他们的主要任务是获得令人满意的学习成绩，以及获得各种技能，作为未来良好

Topic 4　现代人给宠物花的钱太多了？

发展的基础。他们应该购买书籍或参加培训课程，以帮助他们理解在学校学到的课程材料，而不是用他们的津贴或兼职工作收入给宠物消费。此外，他们也很有必要报名参加许多课外活动，包括运动队或辩论俱乐部，在那里他们能够获得各种基本技能，如合作、领导和沟通，所有这些都需要大量的经济投资。然而，今天，我们经常看到学生用他们的零花钱购买宠物玩具或食品，这充分证明他们在宠物上的花费超过了必要的范围，因为他们还有其他更重要的方面需要投资。

## My answer 2

　　我同意 Zoe 的观点。我认为在关爱宠物方面的花费是值得的。许多退休老人通常独自度过他们的大部分日子，因此他们的宠物充当了他们唯一真正的伴侣、朋友，甚至是依靠。以我的邻居为例。他们是一对退休夫妇，他们的孩子已经长大成人并组建了自己的家庭，所以这对老夫妇自己生活。在他们拥有宠物之前，他们的日子常常是枯燥无味的。但是在他们收养了两只狗和一只猫之后，他们的生活就完全改变了。通过饲养这些小动物，这对夫妇逐渐开始认识到他们自己的价值和意义。他们觉得虽然他们不再有工作，但仍有生命需要他们的照顾。同时，这些动物也给这对夫妇带来了无尽的快乐和爱。虽然宠物的日常支出占他们养老金的很大一部分，但这对夫妇的投资肯定是值得的，因为他们发现宠物的存在对他们的疗愈作用极大。

作　者：蒙欢

成绩单：

Your Scores from Test Date:
**October 12, 2021**

| Total (0–120) | Reading (0–30) | Listening (0–30) | Speaking (0–30) | Writing (0–30) |
|---|---|---|---|---|
| 116 | 30 | 28 | 28 | 30 |

# Topic 5
# 现在比过去更容易接受教育吗?

**Section 1 of 1**

Your professor is teaching a class on education. Write a post responding to the professor's question.

**In your response, you should do the following.**
- Express and support your personal opinion.
- Make a contribution to the discussion in your own words.

An effective response will contain at least 100 words.

Professor

Education plays an indispensable role in one's personal success and the long-term development of a country at large. Recently, whether it is easier for people to receive education than it was in the past has drawn wide attention. What is your inclination and why?

Topic 5　现在比过去更容易接受教育？

00:09:59　　Hide Timer

**Samuel**

I think it is easier for people to receive education today than in the past because the Internet is much more advanced than before. If you encounter problems that you need help with, there are many free resources on the Internet that you can refer to, such as YouTube videos, Khan, Wikipedia, etc. The web also facilitates discussions between us, as we are doing. These resources provide us with a lot of convenience, as we can choose any time, any place, any subject for knowledge intake.

**Lisa**

I don't think it is easier for people to receive education than before. More specifically, the pace of society is getting faster and faster, and people have less and less time to really calm down and involve in study. In addition, the depreciation of academic diploma is so severe that many people need to rethink the necessity of going to university to receive education. What's more, the information on the Internet is so much and complicated that it's difficult to tell the true from the false. Not all the information we searched is correct, and some of it can mislead us a lot. This makes education today not as easy as it used to be.

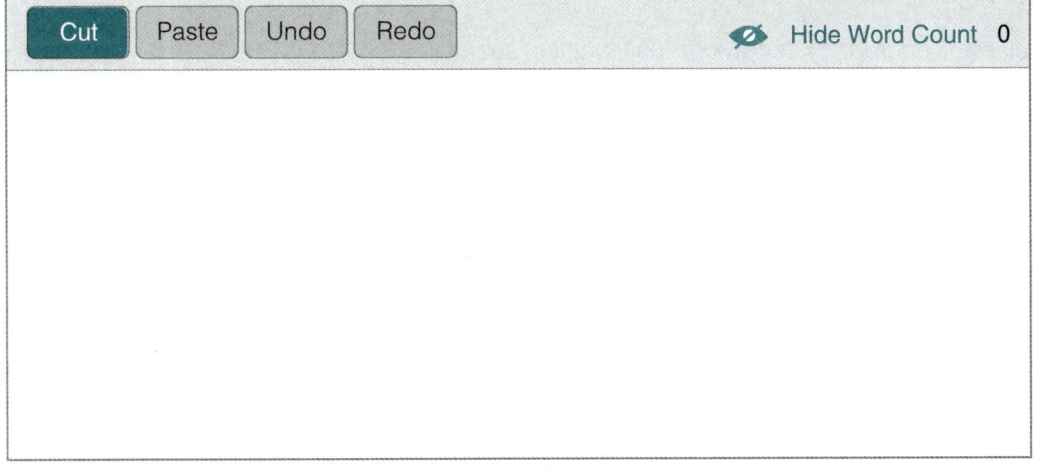

**审题 & 构思**

这个话题非常适合一边倒，承认今天人们接受教育比以前更容易，是更容易上手的论点。

Lisa 的观点也不无道理，道出了客观社会现实。但也非常容易从任何一个角度切入进行反驳。比如，虽然人们变得更忙了，但碎片化的时间也同样意味着可以学习的零碎机会更多，这也是接受教育变容易的体现。学历贬值并不代表大学教育无意义，也不能用大学教育以偏概全地看待整体教育。网上信息冗杂，更锻炼了当今人们的思辨能力，这本身也是教育的一部分。每一个角度都可以论证，今天人们接受教育即便比以往不是更加容易，至少也不会比以往更难。

 **My answer 1**

From my perspective, nowadays, it is indeed easier for people to become educated than their counterparts in the past. To be specific, with the advancement of cutting-edge technologies, people nowadays have easier access to high quality education.[1] With the advent of the Internet, abundant learning resources are available online, which allows people to search for useful information and take open classes without the constraint of time and space.[2] For example, when I was in college, I used to watch open classes offered by renowned universities such as Harvard University and Yale University.[3] Despite the fact that I was a poor girl who lived in China, the Internet enabled me to obtain the best learning resources and gain a deeper insight into my major. However, in the past, such resources were not available. People who lived in remote areas had no access to such learning resources. In fact, only those who came from privileged families had the

[1] 作者给出了原因支持论点，即高科技使得现代人更容易接受教育。

[2] 给出了高科技的细节：互联网的应用、有用的资源和公开课。

[3] 用自己的例子说明在互联网上观看哈佛大学和耶鲁大学公开课的收获。

opportunity to study abroad and receive quality education.⁴ In this sense, it is the rapid development of the Internet that enables average people to receive superior education. (183 words)

| 4 | 分析过去缺少科技资源的情况，证明科技对于教育的重要性。|

## My answer 2

I stand with Samuel's side by adding that with the improvement of living standards, people are financially capable of affording education now,⁵ which makes people easier to receive education. In the past, it was not uncommon that teenagers had to drop out of school to earn their own living and support their family. For them, education is a luxury.⁶ However, with the increase of quality of life, parents do not have to worry about making ends meet and they can afford their children to receive secondary and tertiary education. Many parents are even capable of sending their children abroad for further study. Take my friend Alex for example.⁷ Born with a silver spoon in his mouth, he received excellent private education at a young age. After graduating from high school, he was admitted to New York University as an English major, because his parents, who worked as programmers and earned decent salaries, could afford the expensive tuition fee. Therefore, only when parents could provide adequate financial support could children receive better education. (172 words)

| 5 | 作者给出自己的观点：物质生活条件的富足使得人们可以负担教育开支。|

| 6 | 分析了过去物质生活条件不足，导致孩子们缺少教育的机会。|

| 7 | 给出具体的例子来证明观点：Alex 读私立学校，可以去美国进修，得益于父母的可观收入，现代人物质条件富足，更容易接受到以往接受不到的教育。|

## My answer 3

I take the same point as Samuel does. I want to add that, nowadays, the government also makes it easier for people to receive education.[8] Specifically speaking, in recent decades, the government has carried out a wide range of measures to guarantee that students, be it poor and wealthy, could receive education, ranging from primary to secondary to tertiary education. For example, thanks to the free compulsory education,[9] all children, including those living in mountainous areas, could receive schooling. Moreover, when they graduate from high school, they can use student loans or scholarships provided by the government to finish their college education.[10] However, such policies did not exist in the past, because the government at that time did not have so much financial resources to undertake such a grand project. In this sense, compared to the past, it is the government's financial support that allows people to receive education, which makes people receive education easier than before. (157 words)

[8] 作者给出了自己的观点：政府对于教育做出了贡献。

[9] 政府提供的义务教育，消除了贫富差异对教育的影响。

[10] 给出了政府的第二个角色：提供学生贷款和奖学金计划，段落内部形成并列，证明了本段分论点——政府对教育的重要贡献。

### Words & Phrases

| | |
|---|---|
| cutting-edge 前沿的 | born with a silver spoon in one's mouth 含着银汤匙出生；生而富贵 |
| with the advent of 随着……的到来 | private education 私立教育 |
| renowned 著名的 | decent salaries 体面的薪水 |
| privileged families 特权家庭 | tuition fee 学费 |
| make ends meet 平衡收支 | free compulsory education 免费义务教育 |
| secondary and tertiary education 中等和高等教育 | |

Topic 5　现在比过去更容易接受教育？　041

> 参考译文

Professor

教育对于个人的成功和国家的长远发展均具有不可或缺的作用。最近，关于"人们是否比过去更容易接受教育"的话题，引起了广泛关注。你的倾向是什么？为什么？

Samuel

我认为今天人们比过去更容易接受教育，因为网络比以前发达很多。如果学习中遇到不懂的问题，网络上有很多免费的资源可以参考，比如YouTube视频、可汗学院、维基百科网站等。网络还方便我们之间进行讨论，就像我们正在做的这样。这些资源给我们提供很多方便，我们可以选择任何时间、任何地点、任何主题进行知识摄取。

Lisa

我不认为人们比以前更容易接受教育，社会的发展使得现在人们接受教育比以前更困难了。更具体地说，社会节奏越来越快，人们真正静下心来学习的时间越来越少。另外，学历贬值非常厉害，很多人需要重新思考读大学接受教育的必要性。还有就是，网上的信息又多又杂，真假难辨，我们所查询到的信息未必都是正确的，有的会给我们造成很大的误导，这都使得当今接受教育不如以前简单。

## ■ My answer 1

　　从我的角度来看，现在的人们确实比过去的同龄人更容易接受教育。具体来说，随着尖端技术的进步，人们现在更容易获得高质量的教育。随着互联网的出现，网上有丰富的学习资源，人们可以不受时间和空间的限制，搜索有用的信息、参加公开课程。例如，我上大学的时候，经常观看哈佛大学、耶鲁大学等著名大学的公开课。尽管我是一个生活在中国的穷女孩，但互联网让我获得了最好的学习资源，并让我对自己的专业有了更深入的了解。但是，过去没有这种资源。生活在偏远地区的人们无法获得这样的学习资源。事实上，只有那些来自特权家庭的人才有机会出国留学并接受优质教育。从这个意义上说，正是互联网的快速发展使普通人能够接受更好的教育。

### ■ My answer 2

我同意 Samuel 的观点，并在他的观点上补充说一点：随着生活水平的提高，人们在经济上有能力承担教育，这使得人们比以往更容易接受教育。过去，青少年不得不辍学谋生养家的现象并不少见。对他们来说，教育是一种奢侈品。然而，随着生活质量的提高，父母不必担心入不敷出，他们可以供孩子接受中等和高等教育。许多家长甚至有能力送孩子出国深造。以我的朋友 Alex 为例，含着银汤匙出生的他，很小的时候就读于私立学校。高中毕业后，他考上了纽约大学英语专业，因为他的父母是程序员，收入不错，可以负担昂贵的学费。因此，只有父母能够提供足够的经济支持，孩子才能接受更好的教育。

### ■ My answer 3

我和 Samuel 的观点相同，另外我认为，政府的因素也使人们更容易接受教育。具体来说，近几十年来，政府采取了广泛的措施，以保证学生无论贫富，都能接受从初等到中等到高等的教育。例如，由于免费义务教育，所有的孩子，包括那些生活在山区的孩子，都可以接受教育。此外，当他们高中毕业时，他们可以使用政府提供的学生贷款或奖学金来完成他们的大学教育。但是，这样的政策在过去是不存在的,因为政府当时没有那么多的财力来承担这样一个宏大的项目。从这个意义上说,与过去相比,政府的资金支持让人们能够接受教育,人们比以前更容易接受教育。

作　者:王元元

成绩单:

Your Scores from Test Date:
**October 19, 2021**

| Total<br>(0 – 120) | Reading<br>(0 – 30) | Listening<br>(0 – 30) | Speaking<br>(0 – 30) | Writing<br>(0 – 30) |
|---|---|---|---|---|
| 111 | 28 | 29 | 24 | 30 |

# Topic 6
## 招商引资 or 保护环境，哪个更优先？

**Section 1 of 1**

Your professor is teaching a class on political science. Write a post responding to the professor's question.

**In your response, you should do the following.**
- Express and support your personal opinion.
- Make a contribution to the discussion in your own words.

An effective response will contain at least 100 words.

Dr. Gupta

Today we're going to hold a debate on whether we should spend more money on attracting new business to the city or region than reducing air and water pollution. New businesses can create new jobs and give people money they can use to improve their lives. On the other hand, if we can reduce air and water pollution, it can be enjoyed both by ourselves and future generations. If you had to choose between spending more money on economic growth or protecting the environment, which one would you choose? Why?

Topic 6　招商引资 or 保护环境，哪个更优先？

00:09:59　 Hide Timer

Alex

I would spend more money on reducing air and water pollution. Business opportunities are important, but not at the expense of the environment. Currently, factories are discharging industrial wastes into rivers and automobiles are emitting tons of pollutants into the air. The pollution problem is threatening public health and we need to take immediate actions to protect the environment by putting more investment on controlling pollution levels during industrial protection. In this way, we can enjoy better health and nicer environment.

Maggie

While I agree with Alex that pollution problem needs to be addressed soon, I think the priority should be attracting more businesses into our city, in order to solve poverty and strengthen our economy. Attracting new business can create more jobs, bring in talented people and advanced business models, which can bring long-term economic benefits to our city. With solid financial foundations can we apply modern technologies to deal with pollution problems efficiently and effectively.

| Cut | Paste | Undo | Redo | Hide Word Count 0 |

**审题 & 构思**

这个话题本质上是要钱还是要命的问题，要发展还是要美景的问题，当然也可以兼顾，但是不容易写好。Alex 和 Maggie 都是一边倒地陈述各自观点，我站在我的角度补充了 Alex 的观点。

这道题和 Part 1 里的样题很类似，这里提供两个观点，读者可体会到什么叫"多元化"。

 **My answer 1**

I strongly agree with Alex's idea[1] that putting more money on pollution reduction is important since people are experiencing a wide range of health effects from being exposed to air and river pollution. I would add that[2] high exposure to air and river pollution also endangers animal and plant species, especially those birds and fish living in the vicinity of industrial regions. Maggie raised the relevant point that[3] we need funding to build hi-tech cleaning facilities, but she ignores the fact that many people are experiencing respiratory diseases such as asthma and lung cancer caused by air pollutants, and they cannot wait for decades until we build hi-tech cleaning facilities. Also,[4] promoting regulatory programs to reduce pollution level does not cost millions of dollars to achieve the goal. Instead, cutting pollution can bring financial benefits to the community. For example,[5] the EPA estimates that for every dollar invested in reducing diesel exhaust, a community may achieve up to 13 dollars in public health benefits. Overall, then, I'd say that the government should spend more money on reducing air and water pollution.[6] (181 words)

[1] 先肯定了 Alex 的观点。

[2] 从这里开始才进入题目要求 make a contribution 的节奏。

[3] 通过转述引用 Maggie 的观点，指出其想法的漏洞，继而铺开展示我自己的观点。

[4] 陈述观点时的层次递进。

[5] 光陈述有些干，这里补充一个具体例子，进一步说明我前面的两个论点。一方面有助于凑足至少 100 词的要求，另一方面更能清晰阐述我前面的两个观点。具体例子当中有数据做支撑，使得我的说明有理有据，让人信服。

[6] 最后多一句总结，显得发表的观点结构完整。

## My answer 2

I agree with Maggie[7] when she said that developing economy should be regarded as the top priority[8] since economy serves as the foundation to address other important issues such as education, scientific development and environmental protection. This is especially true[9] in developing countries or elsewhere in economic recessions. When countries suffer dire economic situations, the government needs to put investments on improving people's well-beings in order to protect citizens against hunger and epidemics, creating well-functioned environment for sustainable development.[10] Also,[11] the economic forces leading to change in the composition and techniques of production can exert positive effects on the environment. In fact, only companies with strong economic power are in a position to develop green infrastructures such as water disposal facilities and pollution control services. Therefore,[12] I suggest we put more investments on economic development, both public and private, to facilitate the shift to a low carbon and resource efficient growth. (151 words)

[7] 这是反写的观点。

[8] 列出观点。

[9] 观点的递进。

[10] 进一步解释说明为什么发展经济应列为首要选项。

[11] 二次递进。

[12] 总结观点。

| Words & Phrases | |
|---|---|
| vicinity 附近 | dire 极其严重的 |
| asthma 哮喘病 | infrastructure 基础设施 |
| diesel exhaust 柴油机尾气 | water disposal facilities 水处理的设施 |

## 参考译文

Dr.Gupta 今天我们将就是否应该花更多的钱来为城市或地区吸引新企业而不是减少空气和水污染的问题进行讨论。新企业可以创造新的就业机会,并为人们提供可用于改善生活的资金。另一方面,如果我们能够减少空气和水污染,我们和子孙后代都可以享受到对应的福利。如果你需要在增加经济增长和保护环境之间做一个选择,你会选择哪一个?为什么?

Alex 我会选择花更多的钱来减少空气和水污染。商业机会固然重要,但不能以牺牲环境为代价。目前,工厂正在向河流排放工业废物,汽车正在向空气中排放成吨的污染物。污染问题正在威胁公众的健康,我们需要立即采取行动保护环境,在工业保护的同时加大对控制污染水平的资金投入。这样,我们就可以拥有更好的健康(水平)和更好的环境。

Maggie 虽然我同意 Alex 的观点,即污染问题需要尽快解决,但我认为首要任务应该是吸引更多企业进入我们的城市,以解决贫困问题并强化我们的经济基础。招商引资可以创造更多的就业岗位,引进人才和先进的商业模式,可以为我市带来长远的经济效益。有了坚实的财政基础,我们才能应用现代技术,高效、有效地处理污染问题。

### ▎My answer 1

我非常同意 Alex 的观点,即在减少污染方面投入更多的资金很重要,因为暴露于空气和河流污染中正对人们的健康产生广泛影响。我要补充的是,长期暴露于空气和河流污染中也会危及动植物物种,尤其是生活在工业区附近的鸟类和鱼类。Maggie 提出了我们需要资金来建设高科技清洁设施的相关观点,但她忽略了一个事实,即许多人正在经历空气污染物引起的呼吸道疾病,例如哮喘和肺癌,他们等不及几十年后才能建成高科技清洁设施。此外,推动降低污染水平的监管计划并不需要花费数百万美元来实现对应目标。相反,减少污染可以为社区带来经济利益。例如,据美国环保署估计，在减少柴油机尾气方面每投资一美元，一个社区可能会获得高达 13 美元的公共卫生效益。总的来说，我会认为政府应该花更多的钱来减少空气和水污染。

### My answer 2

我同意 Maggie 的观点，因为她提到发展经济应该放在首要位置。经济毕竟是解决像教育、科研、环境保护等其他重要问题的基础。发展经济对发展中国家或正处于经济萧条的地区更是重要。当国家的经济状况非常糟糕时，政府更应该加大投资，以提高民众的福祉，避免他们陷入饥饿和流行病，并且为他们创造美好的、可持续发展的环境。此外，导致生产构成和技术发生变化的经济力量可以对环境产生积极的影响。事实上只有那些具有强大经济实力的公司才能愿意发展绿色基础设施，例如水处理设施和污染控制服务。因此，我主张在经济发展上面投入更多资源，这样于公于私都有道理，以促进（经济模式）向低碳和资源高效增长的转变。

作　者：薛白
成绩单：

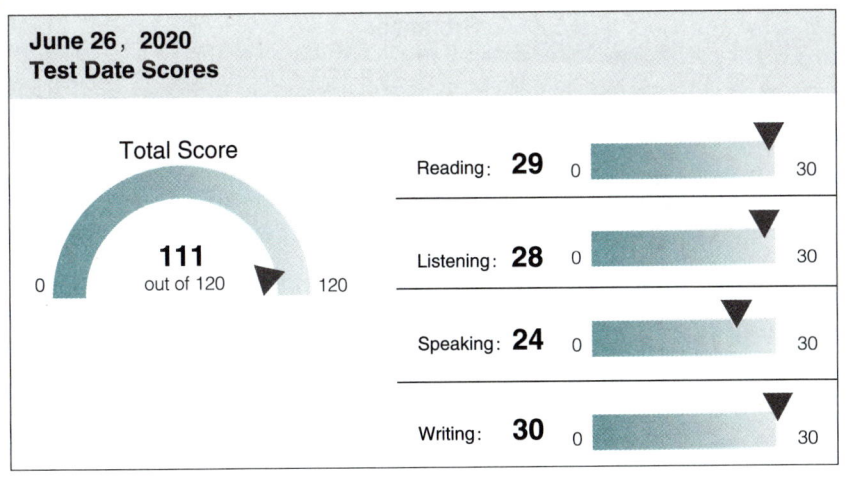

# Topic 7
## 在国内 or 出国研学旅行？

Section 1 of 1

Your professor is teaching a class on education. Write a post responding to the professor's question.

**In your response, you should do the following.**
- Express and support your personal opinion.
- Make a contribution to the discussion in your own words.

An effective response will contain at least 100 words.

Professor

A school trip is always welcomed in midst of all the lectures and tests in school. If given the opportunity to be away for a week and write a paper about it, would you prefer to spend that week in a location in your own country that you have not visited before, or would you prefer to spend the week in a location in another country? Why?

Topic 7　在国内 or 出国研学旅行?

00:09:59　 Hide Timer

Michael

I would like to spend a week in a location in my own country for my school trip. As a student, my pocket money is limited, and I need to be pragmatic when making choices. There are many advantages of choosing a location in my own country for a school trip, such as saving travel expenses, no language barrier, and being closer to the actual content I learned in class. In contrast, if I choose to go to another country for a school trip, the travel expenses will definitely not be cheap, and the visa will also be troublesome. If I am not familiar with the place, the overall favorability of the trip will be compromised.

Jenny

Michael's choice seems logical, but I still want to spend my school trip time in another country that I have not visited before. Staying in one environment for a long time will naturally narrow one's vision, and a school trip is a good opportunity to get to know and contact the outside world, and understand that what we have learned in class can be applied to a wider world. This will make us more motivated when we return to the classroom. Now that the Covid 19 epidemic is over, globalization has entered a new stage. Only by better understanding the outside world can we better think about the meaning of our lives.

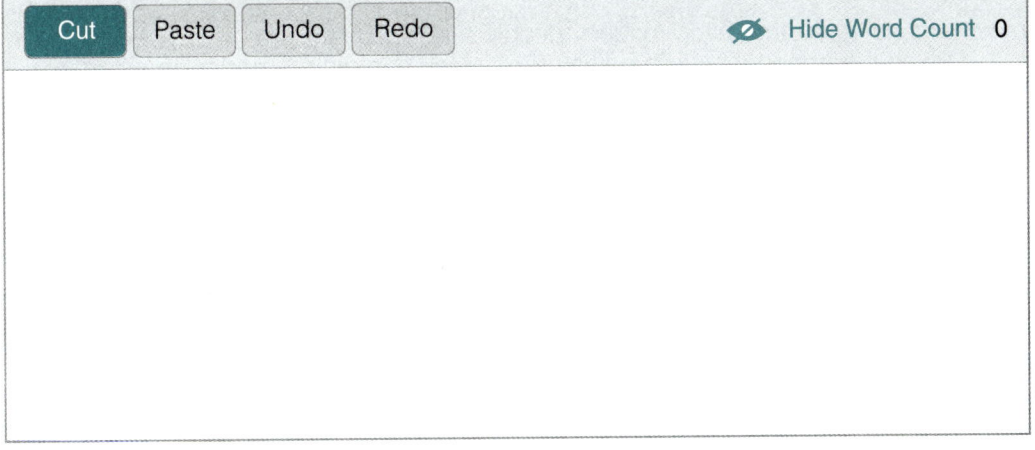

## 审题 & 构思

这道题的目的是需要论述选择在国内还是去国外旅游来完成自己的一篇旅游心得文章，我选择在首都北京旅游，因为我可以从它的历史、现代化等角度去探访并书写。

历史方面，北京是著名的历史古都，其中长城的历史价值值得书写。另外，我对故宫的建筑很感兴趣，所以考虑用9999.5个房间的传说作为细节让文章更生动。

北京也有现代化的一面，鉴于抖音的火爆我觉得走访抖音总部能给我提供很多素材。考虑到作答时间，我只能切入其中一个角度进行论述，所以我提供两个例子作答。

## My answer 1

Michael speaks my mind. A school trip place in my own country, say Beijing, China, is not a worse choice if compared with a destination in another country. To elaborate more, Beijing is rich in Chinese history,[1] which is good material to write about. Name all the famous places I'm so familiar with from high school history text books: the Forbidden City, the Summer Palace, the Great Wall…[2] All these household names reside in Beijing. I would go to the Great Wall to see the great piece of achievement by my ancestors with *primitive* tools thousands of years ago on mountains so steep that even modern people find it difficult to *erect* buildings on.[3] Also, I would love to visit the Forbidden City, the residence of emperors of Ming and Qing dynasties. The Forbidden City has so many tales, real or fictional, about it. Any one of them will be interesting to write and read. A school trip can be no less meaningful if the place is fed with history, and it is more likely that we get familiar with a local school trip place better.[4] (186 words)

**1** 论点给出了选择北京的理由：历史，下文的写作目的是对北京历史展开详细解释。

**2** 进一步给出具体的北京地点，结合历史特点。

**3** 解释长城的细节。

**4** 考试时，由于时间受限，写到这里就可以了，而且已经很难得了。下面这一段加了【】，可做参考，都写上肯定是写不完的。但如果想围绕Forbidden City这个小点展开，前面可以省略一些关于 Great Wall 的文字，为Forbidden City这段文字留足打字的时间。

【For example, it is said that the Forbidden City consists of 9,999.5 rooms, which is only one room less than 10,000. The reason lies in the interesting fact that 10,000 is believed to be the number of rooms in Heavenly Palace, the residence by Chinese supreme deity. In order to show humility, the earthly emperors have the rooms deliberately less.⁵ I would love to check the story out to see if the number is correct and maybe investigate in my writing the relationship between Chinese emperors and deities.⁶】(88 more words)

**5** 给出非常具体的关于紫禁城的历史小故事，来突出作者的观点——历史悠久。需要特别注意，作者给出了数字，三位用逗号分隔，这点和中文习惯不同；通过关于天宫的传说，清楚地解释了紫禁城的有趣小传说，这些都紧扣本段论点——rich in history。

**6** 结尾作者自然扣题，与上文例子衔接自然，也回应了题目，整个段落流畅。

## 📄 My answer 2

I prefer to pitch in a school trip that is in my own country. I would like to visit and write about the modern parts of Beijing,⁷ the capital city of my country. The city, like its counterparts in U.S. or U.K., has exciting skyscrapers and tech parks, which house world famous tech companies with employees graduated from top-tier universities globally. Tik-Tok is the most famous one. The headquarters of Tick-tock are located in Haidian District, the tech hub of Beijing.⁸ I would visit the Tik-Tok headquarters to see how engineers there create a video service which attracts users around the world and include my observations in my writing. Since my country already has these high-tech elements worthy of my visit and writing, there is no need for me to go to a place abroad for a school trip.⁹ (138 words)

**7** 作者展开自己的论点：突出北京的现代性，和 My answer 1 里面呈现的角度不同。

**8** 进一步解释现代北京，高科技企业 Tick-Tok。

**9** 细节回答，联系讨论的题目。

### Words & Phrases

| | |
|---|---|
| primitive 原始的 | top-tier universities 一流大学 |
| erect 建造 | tech hub 技术中心 |
| deity 神 | |

> 参考译文

Professor

在学校的所有讲座和考试中，学校旅行总是受欢迎。如果有机会离开一个星期并写一篇关于它的论文，那一周你愿意在你自己国家的一个你以前没有去过的地方度过，还是你愿意在另一个国家的某个地方度过？为什么？

Michael

我愿意在我自己国家的一个地方花一个星期完成我的学校旅行。作为学生，我的零花钱有限，做选择需要务实。选择一个我自己国家的地方进行学校旅行有很多好处，比如节省路费、没有语言障碍、更贴近我在课堂上学到的实际内容。对比起来，如果选择去另外一个国家进行学校旅行，路费一定不会便宜，签证也会很麻烦，人生地不熟，整体旅程的好感会打折扣。

Jenny

Michael 的观点听起来是有逻辑的，但我还是想把我的学校旅行放到一个我没去过的境外国家。长时间待在一个环境里，一个人的视野会自然变窄，而学校旅行是个很好的机会，认识、接触外面的世界，理解我们在课堂上所学的东西可以应用到更广阔的世界，这会使我们回到课堂后学习更有动力。现如今疫情已经结束，全球化进入一个新阶段，只有更好地了解外面的世界才能更好地思考自己生活的意义。

## ■ My answer 1

　　Michael 说出了我的心声。在我自己国家选择一个地方进行学校旅行，比如北京，至少不会比在境外选择一个地方要差。进一步讲，北京有丰富的中国历史，这是很好的写作素材。如果列举一些高中历史课本上我熟悉的名胜：紫禁城、颐和园、长城……这些家喻户晓的名字都来自北京。我会去长城，看我的祖先在几千年前用原始工具在陡峭的山上所取得的伟大成就，即使是现代人也很难在上面建造建筑物。此外，我还想去参观故宫，它是明、清两代皇帝的居所。紫禁城有很多关于它的故事，真实的或虚构的。它们中的任何一个都将是有趣的写作和阅读主题。如果一个地方富有历史意义，去这个地方进行学校旅行就会是有意义的，我们也很可能会对学校旅行的地点更了解。

【例如，据说紫禁城由9999.5个房间组成，只比10000个房间少半个房间。原因在于一个有趣的事实，10000被认为是天宫里房间的数量，天宫是中国神仙的住所。为了表示谦虚，人间的皇帝故意把房间弄得更少。我很想验证一下这个传说，看看数字是否正确，也想在我的文章中探讨一下中国皇帝和神灵之间的关系。】

## My answer 2

我倾向于参与一个在我自己国家的学校旅行。我想参观并写写北京的现代部分。北京是我国的首都城市。这座城市，就像美国或英国的城市一样，拥有令人兴奋的摩天大楼和科技园区，其中有世界著名的科技公司，里面的员工毕业于世界上很多顶级大学。Tik-Tok 是（这里）最著名的科技公司，它的总部位于北京科技中心海淀区。我会去 Tik-Tok 总部，看看那里的工程师是如何创建一个吸引世界各地用户的视频服务的，并把我的观察写进我的文章里。既然我的国家已经有这些值得我参观和写作的高科技元素，我就没有必要在国外进行学校旅行了。

作　者：史禺

成绩单：

Your Scores from Test Date:
**November 02, 2021**

| Total<br>(0 – 120) | Reading<br>(0 – 30) | Listening<br>(0 – 30) | Speaking<br>(0 – 30) | Writing<br>(0 – 30) |
|---|---|---|---|---|
| 110 | 29 | 30 | 23 | 28 |

# Topic 8
## 自主阅读比老师留的阅读作业重要？

Section 1 of 1

Your professor is teaching a class on reading. Write a post responding to the professor's question.

**In your response, you should do the following.**
- Express and support your personal opinion.
- Make a contribution to the discussion in your own words.

An effective response will contain at least 100 words.

Professor

The importance of reading is beyond doubt. From kindergartens to universities, teachers and professors are inclined to assign reading tasks to students in order to make them better informed and educated. Here comes the question: Is this kind of reading more important than the reading that a student does on his or her own? Please give your opinion and let's start the talk.

# Topic 8　自主阅读比老师留的阅读作业重要？

00:09:59　Hide Timer

James

I think reading that a student does on his or her own weighs more than reading assigned by teachers. The thing is, if the students choose the books on their own, it is more likely that the books suit their interest. This makes a huge difference: actively reading something that one is interested in makes the whole process more productive, because only by doing so can a student be fully devoted into reading, instead of rushing to complete a "homework". He or she may underline the important parts, search for information regarding specific information in the book, write down personal reflection of the book, and even share the knowledge or story with his or her friends.

Margaret

Reading assignments from the teachers are important and necessary as students are not mature enough to choose their own reading: they will simply choose cheap entertaining material instead of the truly useful books, while teachers are the "sheepherders" to make sure that they make the right choice. Grown up in the information era, filled with guidance to show them a not that clear path, students are not mature enough to make their own judgement. Students may choose futile or superficial stuff unless offered with help from their teachers or professors.

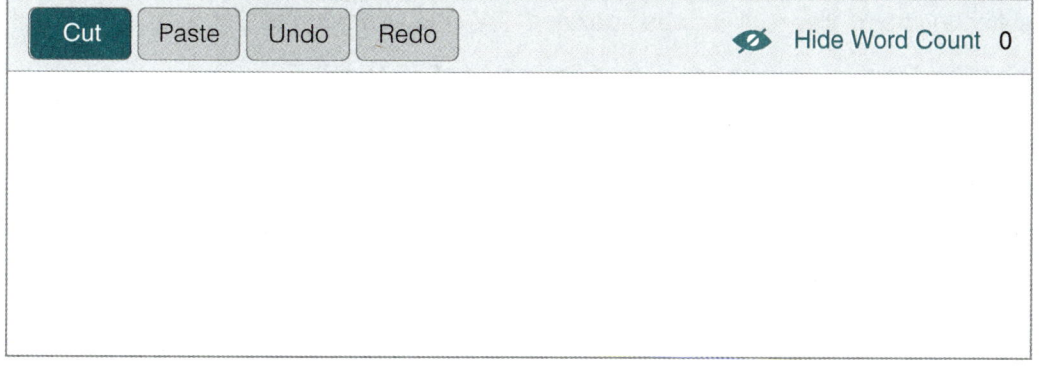

### 审题 & 构思

本题为标准的比较类题目，即问两类事物孰优孰劣，比较的对象为学生自主阅读和老师规定的阅读。拿到这类题目后，作者会先比较双方的优劣，哪边的优势更明显，更好解释，更好配例子，作者就支持哪边。这个话题存在 A 和 B 两面，都可以切入。作者倾向于学生选择自己喜欢读的书，可以列举两个理由，写成两篇范文。

James 亮明观点：认为学生自主选择的书更匹配自身兴趣。进一步给出细节：全身心投入阅读和完成作业的差异巨大。最后给出关于自主阅读的更多细节，详细解释其包括的内容：标注、搜索相关信息、反思和分析。

Margaret 的观点与我选择的方向相反，但 Margaret 在这里已经说得比较全了，所以比较难再从她的选择方向补充内容。读者可以发挥想象力，看看自己有没有可能在这个基础上再补充一些个人观点，凑上至少 100 词。

### My answer 1

I would like to add more to James's point by taking me as an example.[1] When I was in junior high school, my English teacher authorized students to choose our own books for the summer vacation's reading assignment. **Intrigued by** the topic and tone, I chose to read *The Fault on the Stars*, a very popular love story between two teenagers suffering from illness.[2] I was dazzled by the book's **elaborate diction**, **beautiful personification** and **thought-provoking ending**, which combined, created the most perfect reading experience of my life.[3] If I had been forced to read something that I am not interested in, I would have lost this beautiful experience. Other people may not share this enthusiasm for love story. For a boy who enjoys space

[1] 对于本题而言，作者认为自主阅读的优势更好阐述，可以着重强调兴趣的重要性。James 已经把道理讲得比较清楚，也就是阐述为什么有兴趣的主动阅读能够产生更好的效果，作者在自己的作答中，再配上充足的示例去补充。

[2] 作者给出自己的亲身阅读经历。

[3] 带来的效果印证了本段论点。

fantasy and imaginative otherworldly descriptions, science fictions like *Dune* or *The Three-Body Problem* are obviously the better choice.⁴ (143 words)

4 进一步给出其他书籍匹配不同兴趣，加强了本段的说服力。

 **My answer 2**

I hold a similar viewpoint as James does. The benefit of the reading that a student does on his or her own is that people differ from one another the way books do.⁵ In other words, there is not a single book that can suit the need of everybody in the world, especially in terms of utilitarian benefits. If a student looks forward to challenging himself or herself in the business field in the future, he or she should choose the autobiography of successful businesspeople like Mr. Buffet, improving sensitivity to the fluctuations in the market; if a prospect politics student wants to know more about the structure of the government and how it works, books like *The Federalists Papers* are the preferred choice; if a student has an ambitious dream of becoming the next Nobel Prize winner of physics, Stephen Hawking's *A Brief History of Time* will be the best gateway to the wonders of the universe.⁶ (158 words)

5 作者给出了学生自主阅读的好处——彼此不同。

6 具体列出了不同的自主阅读领域：巴菲特的自传、《联邦党人文集》和《时间简史》，具体解释不同在哪里。当然这里列举的书名比较专业，读者可以替换为自己熟悉的其他书籍名称，用自己熟悉的例子去论证，最好是自己真看过的书籍，才能讲得更深入。

| Words & Phrases | |
|---|---|
| be fully devoted into 全心投入 | thought-provoking ending 发人深省的结局 |
| intrigued by 被吸引 | otherworldly descriptions 超凡脱俗的描述 |
| elaborate diction 精心的措辞 | utilitarian 实用的 |
| beautiful personification 美丽的拟人化 | autobiography 自传 |

## 参考译文

Professor

阅读的重要性毋庸置疑。从幼儿园到大学，教师和教授都倾向于将阅读任务布置给学生，以使他们更好地了解知识和受教育。问题来了：这种阅读是否比学生自主阅读更重要？请发表你的意见，让我们开始讨论。

James

我认为学生自己选择愿意读的书去读，比老师安排其去读对应的书更重要。事实上，如果学生自己选择书籍，书更有可能符合他们的兴趣。这就产生了巨大的不同：积极地阅读自己感兴趣的东西会使整个过程更有成效，因为只有这样学生才能完全投入到阅读中，而不是急于完成"家庭作业"。他们可能会在重要的部分画线，在书中搜索有关的特定信息，写下对这本书的个人反思，甚至与朋友分享知识或故事。

Margaret

老师安排给学生的阅读任务是重要且必要的，因为学生还不够成熟去选择他们该阅读的东西。他们只会选择廉价的娱乐材料，而不是真正有用的书，而老师是"牧羊人"，以确保他们做出正确的选择。学生成长在信息时代，到处都是不是那么清晰的路径指引，学生们还不足以成熟到可以做出自己的正确判断。学生很可能选择无用或肤浅的东西，除非老师或教授给他们必要的帮助。

### ■ My answer 1

我愿意以我为例，在 James 的观点基础上补充说一些内容。在我上初中的时候，我的英语老师让学生们自己选择书作为暑假阅读作业。因为被主题和语气所吸引，我选择了读《星星的错》，这是一个非常流行的爱情故事，讲述的是两个身患疾病的青少年之间的故事。我被这本书精心的措辞、美丽的拟人化和发人深省的结局所折服，这些结合在一起，创造了我一生中最完美的阅读体验。如果我被迫读一些我不感兴趣的东西，我就会失去这种美好的经历。其他人可能不会对爱情故事有同样的热情。对于一个喜欢太空幻想和富有想象力的超凡脱俗的描述的男孩来说，像《沙丘》或《三体》这样的科幻小说显然是更好的选择。

## My answer 2

　　我和 James 的观点相似。学生自己阅读的另一个好处是，人与人之间的差异就像书籍之间的差异一样。换句话说，没有一本书能满足世界上所有人的需要，特别是在功利利益方面。如果学生希望将来在商业领域挑战自我，应该选择像巴菲特这样的成功商人的自传，提高对市场波动的敏感度；如果一名政治学专业的学生想了解更多关于政府的结构及其工作原理，《联邦党人文集》之类的书籍是首选；如果一个学生有成为下一个诺贝尔物理学奖得主的远大梦想，斯蒂芬·霍金的《时间简史》将是通往宇宙奇迹的最佳门户。

作　者：刘仁谦
成绩单：

Your Scores from Test Date:
**September 21, 2021**

| Total (0–120) | Reading (0–30) | Listening (0–30) | Speaking (0–30) | Writing (0–30) |
|---|---|---|---|---|
| 115 | 30 | 29 | 29 | 27 |

# Topic 9
## 分任务完成 or 一起完成小组作业?

**Section 1 of 1**

Your professor is teaching a class on education. Write a post responding to the professor's question.

**In your response, you should do the following.**
- Express and support your personal opinion.
- Make a contribution to the discussion in your own words.

An effective response will contain at least 100 words.

Professor

Group projects are an essential part of everyday life in school. Here comes the question: Is it better to work independently, separating the quest equally into different parts, with each member responsible to his or her own part only, or is it better to collaborate in every step of the process? What is your take?

00:09:59   Hide Timer

Smith

I prefer to work independently while doing a group project as I am concerned about the possible occurrence of free-riding if students choose to collaborate in the whole process. After all, not everyone is responsible in his or her own part, it is highly possible for the "free rider" to simply rely on the efforts of other people without contributing to the team. Unless extra mechanism can be arranged to prevent free-riding from happening (for example, teachers can let team members grade each other's contribution to the team), otherwise, I could not trust the achievements done by collaboration between students while doing a group project.

Zoe

I see your point, Smith, but I prefer to work collaboratively when doing a group project. My experience serves as a precise example. When I was in junior high school, two of my classmates and I were assigned to deliver a survey regarding students' opinion towards the cafeteria renovation program. We drew the initial plan together, decided the exact method of surveying students together, processed the data together, and wrote the report together. Even if there was a disagreement among us, we expressed our idea, tried to reach a compromise, and learned from each other in the process. In the end, we delivered an eminent presentation in front of the class, receiving applauses and an "A+". This is one of the best experiences in my life, and I benefit from it even until now.

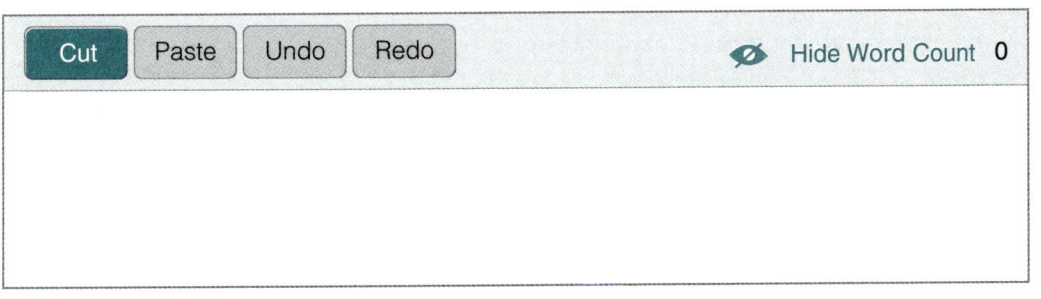

### 审题 & 构思

本题为标准的比较类题目，即问两类事物孰优孰劣，比较的对象为小组成员各司其职还是大家一起通力合作。拿到这类题目后，我会先比较双方的优劣，哪边的优势更明显，更好解释，更好配例子，我就支持哪边。

对于本题而言，我认为通力合作的优势更好阐述，如文章所述，可以着重强调通力合作会避免各司其职的一个关键隐患：最终分数与自己的贡献不匹配。这个逻辑较为复杂，需要阐述清晰，并强调拿到公平结果的重要性。另外，在第二篇范文中，我强调合作交流能力的锻炼，这可以视为一个新版托福写作中的万能理由，在很多题目中都适用。

Smith 指出了团队合作可能存在的问题，如"搭便车效应"，即可能会有成员自己不努力工作，但能坐享其成。Smith 的担忧不无道理，读者可以顺着这个思路继续补充，也可以揪住这个思路里可以反驳的点进行扩展辩驳。

Zoe 表达了和 Smith 不同的观点。Zoe 用自己读初中时参与的一个合作项目来举例，证明团队合作对个人的帮助。通过后面的具体事例里的亮点词语，读者可体会 Zoe 在聊天板上展现出的语言厚度。

### My answer 1

I believe Zoe's point is more reasonable since most teachers will grade the students as a group, instead of grading them individually, so the mechanism of holding each student responsible for one part is unfair for some students.[1] Let me explain. It is fairly common that students of different academic level team up together, so the result of the previously mentioned mechanism is clear: Some parts of the project may end up being a very satisfactory result, other parts not so excellent. The teacher will have to give the whole group an average grade, which clearly fails to reflect the performance of individual students.[2] On the

[1] 开头亮出自己的观点：同意 Zoe 的观点。since 之后的内容是补充的具体理由，与题目里要求的 "make a contribution" 相呼应；其中提到，如果每位成员各自负责一部分工作，对于有些学生来说不太公平。

[2] 解释论证：具体说明不公平的原因：每个同学的学术水平不同，如果每个成员各自负责一部分工作，完成质量会参差不齐，最终给出的平均分并不能很好地反应每个成员的水平。

Topic 9 分任务完成 or 一起完成小组作业?

other hand,³ if all members collaborate throughout the whole project, the students with better academic abilities will be able to monitor every step of the way, giving suggestions and modifying the flaws. In this way, these top-notch students will have better chance getting a result that fits their level. (155 words)

**3** 进一步对比,团队合作如何能保证能力较强的成员拿到自己满意的分数。

全篇 155 词,展开得当,篇幅合理,是一篇标准限时作答的文章。

## 📝 My answer 2

Zoe raises an interesting point and I want to add that textbook knowledge is not the only thing that students come to schools to study. Communication and collaboration skills, essential skills in the professional world, are also the reason why the Zoe's point is much sounder.⁴ To be specific, no matter what jobs students take in the future, they must communicate and collaborate well with their customers, and more importantly, colleagues. Programmers need to communicate with project managers; designers need to communicate with engineers; financial analysts need to communicate with accountants.⁵ If the students do not have a chance to practice communication and collaboration in school, they may be outcompeted in the job market or marginalized in the company. Thus, collaboration while doing a group project, revolving around communication and collaboration, suits their needs perfectly. (135 words)

**4** 也是开头亮明观点:认同 Zoe 的观点。但从另外一个角度进行补充:通过合作的方式,同学们还能学到重要的职场技能。

**5** 在围绕自己的论点进行解释的同时,列举了一些不同行业的工作,来展示沟通合作的重要性。整篇 135 词,在考试限时规定情况下是可行的作答模板。

| Words & Phrases | |
|---|---|
| free-riding 搭便车 | reach a compromise 达成妥协 |
| renovation 翻新 | top-notch 卓越的 |
| initial plan 初步计划 | be outcompeted in the job market or marginalized in the company 在就业市场上被超越或在公司被边缘化 |

参考译文

Professor

小组作业是学校日常生活的重要组成部分。问题来了：是将任务平均分成不同的部分，每个成员只对自己的部分负责，独立完成更好，还是在过程的每一步都进行协作更好？你怎么看？

Smith

我倾向于独立完成小组作业，因为我担心如果学生选择在整个过程中合作，可能会出现"搭便车"的情况。毕竟，不是每个人都会对自己负责的那部分任务尽心，因此实际操作中很可能会出现这样的"搭便车者"——仅仅指望他人的努力，自己不做贡献。除非这个问题可以通过额外的机制来解决（比如，教师可以让团队成员们互相对其做出的贡献进行打分），否则，我不会相信学生在完成小组任务过程中，通过合作完成的成就。

Zoe

我看到了你的观点，Smith，但我倾向于通过合作方式完成小组作业。拿我自己来举例：在我上初中的时候，我和我的两个同学被指派进行一项调查，是关于学生对食堂改造计划的看法。我们一起制订了最初的计划，一起决定了调查学生的确切方法，一起处理数据，一起写报告。即使我们之间有分歧，我们也表达了各自的想法，进行必要的妥协并达成一致。在整个过程中，我们相互学习。最后，我们在全班同学面前做了一次优秀的演讲，获得了许多掌声和"A+"的好成绩。这是我一生中最好的经历之一，直到现在我都从中受益。

## My answer 1

我认为 Zoe 的观点听起来更靠谱，因为大多数教师会将小组作为一个整体进行评分，而不是对小组成员单独进行评分，因此让每个学生对一部分项目负责的机制对一些学生来说是不公平的。具体来说，不同学术水平的学生一起工作是相当普遍的，因此前面提到的机制结果很明显：项目的某些部分可能会得到一个令人满意的结果，而其他部分则不那么优秀。老师会给整个小组打一个平均分，这显然无法反映个别学生的表现。另一方面，如果所有成员在整个项目中合作，具有更好学术能力的学生将能够监控每一步，提出建议并修改缺陷。这样，这些顶尖的学生将有更好的机会获得符合他们水平的结果。

### ■ My answer 2

　　Zoe 的观点很有意思，我想补充说明的是：课本知识并不是学生到学校学习的唯一目的。沟通和协作技能是职场的基本技能，也是 Zoe 的观点听起来更合理的原因。具体来说，无论学生将来从事什么工作，他们都必须与客户和同事进行良好的沟通和协作。程序员需要与项目经理沟通；设计师需要与工程师沟通；财务分析师需要与会计沟通。如果学生没有机会在学校锻炼沟通和协作能力，他们在职场上就不会有竞争力，甚至会在公司里被边缘化。因此，以合作的方式完成小组作业，围绕沟通和协作，更符合他们的需求。

作　者：刘仁谦

成绩单：

Your Scores from Test Date:
**October 26, 2021**

| Total<br>(0–120) | Reading<br>(0–30) | Listening<br>(0–30) | Speaking<br>(0–30) | Writing<br>(0–30) |
|---|---|---|---|---|
| 114 | 29 | 30 | 28 | 27 |

# Topic 10
## 分任务完成 or 一起完成小组作业?

Section 1 of 1

Your professor is teaching a class on education. Write a post responding to the professor's question.

**In your response, you should do the following.**
- Express and support your personal opinion.
- Make a contribution to the discussion in your own words.

An effective response will contain at least 100 words.

Professor

This term we will have a project as part of the term grade. You are supposed to work on a project with two other students. You can organize the work required for this project in two ways. The first way is working independently, which means that you and the other two students divide the work into three parts so that you are responsible for your part only. Or you may be collaborating with the two other students, which means that you meet with them and complete all parts of the project together. Which approach do you think is better for you? Why?

Topic 10　分任务完成 or 一起完成小组作业?　069

00:09:59　　Hide Timer

**William**

I think it would be better to work alone. In this way, I can handle the work in the way I like. I can have different working hours and work schedules. I don't have to worry about being interrupted by others, and dealing with problems on our own is a very meaningful gain.

**Vivian**

I think it's better to work with two other students. Because everyone is good at something, their knowledge can be used to solve a practical problem if the project is very complex. In addition, the team working atmosphere is very good, more relaxed. One person's work is monotonous and boring.

| Cut | Paste | Undo | Redo | Hide Word Count 0 |

## 审题 & 构思

这道题目属于比较简单的教育类话题，发问的对象也是属于常见的小组合作和个人单干。小组合作是较好入手的角度，因为此合作类的话题可以拓展到职场、科学家之间，甚至不同政府之间。

对于合作的具体内容，则需要展开时给出具体内容，分类讨论；亦可以对学生群体、学科类别进行分类，这样可以做到言之有物。

## My answer 1

I stand with Vivian. Since students could gather together and discuss some tough issues, they are more likely to come up with some brilliant ideas and tackle the problems. Moreover, they might be able to double-check their team members' work, and some mistakes could be noticed and corrected. In sharp contrast, when students divide the task and start to work on the project independently, they tend to pay more attention to their own part instead of exchanging ideas and discussing with the others. Hence, they might have little knowledge about their team members' parts and cannot identify and correct errors, which might affect the quality of the work.

When I was a university student,[1] I was assigned to prepare a presentation about foreign cultures with two other students. We booked a group meeting room in the school library and stayed there for four days, and the structure of the presentation was discussed. It turned out that we did find some mistakes in one chart and some inaccurate information in the descriptions, for each of us checked the slides twice. If we simply divided the project and worked individually on one part of it at home, we might fail to find

[1] 举例论证：通过本人学生时期的经历证明观点。需要注意例子中相关细节的呈现：研究对象、会议室、四天、发现问题。这些细节使例子更生动、具体、可信。

但如果打字速度不够快，从这里开始到段尾的内容可以省略。大家是不是觉得加上这段个人事例说明会比较好？那就训练一下打字速度吧。

out these mistakes, as we spent most of the time working on our share of the work. (217 words)

 **My answer 2**

Vivian speaks my voice. I would add that as students spend most of their time working on one project, which provides more opportunities for interactions and discussions about their personal experience and interests, they will gradually be familiar with each other and then develop a friendship. On the contrary, if students work on different parts of the task, there will be a significant decrease in the time they spend together. It is reasonable that they cannot be acquaint with each other and build a good rapport that can nurture a friendship. My own experience could fully illustrate this point.[2] When I was in high school, I believed that I could excel in different subjects; thus, I suggested that teachers should divide the task and the grade should be given based on each student's performance. Although I got good grades, I was unfamiliar with my team members. I had no idea about their hobbies and preferences, and we could only meet each other several times before giving the presentation. If I could collaborate with them and discuss the tough issue with them together, I could get to know them and developing a friendship with them would be achievable. (197 words)

[2] 举例论证：通过本人学生时期的经历证明观点。因为缺乏彼此之间的沟通与合作，团队成员之间并没有建立友谊，是一大遗憾。

| Words & Phrases | |
|---|---|
| come up with 想出 | be acquaint with 熟悉 |
| tackle the problems 解决问题 | build a good rapport 建立良好的关系 |
| double-check 复核 | collaborate with 与……合作 |
| inaccurate 不准确的 | |

参考译文

Professor

这学期我们会有一个项目作为学期成绩的一部分。你应该和另外两个同学一起做一个项目。你可以通过两种方式组织此项目的工作。第一个方式是独立工作，这意味着你和其他两个同学把工作分成三个部分，你只负责你的部分。或者你可以和另外两个同学合作，这意味着你和他们见面，一起完成项目的所有部分。你认为哪种方法更适合你？为什么？

Willian

我觉得独自工作比较好。这样，我就可以用我喜欢的方式来处理工作了。我可以有不同的工作时间和工作安排。（这样）我就不必担心被别人打断，自己处理问题是一个非常有意义的收获。

Vivian

我觉得和另外两个同学一起工作比较好。因为每个人都有擅长的东西，如果项目非常复杂，他们的（专长）知识可以用来解决实际问题。另外，团队工作的氛围很好，比较轻松，一个人的工作会显得单调乏味。

## My answer 1

　　我同意 Vivian 的观点。如果同学之间选择合作完成任务，聚在一起讨论一些棘手的问题，他们更有可能想出一些绝妙的主意并解决问题。此外，他们或许能够仔细检查团队成员的工作，发现并纠正一些错误。与之形成鲜明对比的是，如果学生分头去完成任务的话，他们往往更关注自己的部分，而不是与他人交换意见和讨论。因此，他们可能对团队成员的（具体）工作知之甚少，无法识别和纠正（他们的）错误，这可能会影响工作的质量。

　　当我是一名大学生时，我被安排与另外两名同学一起准备关于外国文化的演讲。我们在学校图书馆订了一个小组会议室，在那里待了四天，讨论了演讲的结构。结果我们确实发现了一张图表中的一些错误和描述中的一些不准确信息，因为我们每个人都检查了两次 PPT。如果我们只是简单地把项目分开，在家里单独处理自己的那一部分，我们可能就不会发现这些错误，因为我们大部分时间都花在了我们自己的那部分工作上。

## My answer 2

我同意 Vivian 的观点，我想补充的是：由于学生将大部分时间花在一个项目上，这为他们提供了更多互动和讨论个人经历和兴趣的机会，他们将逐渐熟悉彼此并建立友谊。相反，如果学生完成任务的不同部分，他们在一起的时间就会大大减少。可以理解的是，（这样的话）他们就无法相知，无法建立起可以培养友谊的融洽关系。我自己的经历可以充分说明这一点。当我在读高中时，我认为我可以在不同的科目中脱颖而出；因此，我建议老师划分任务，并且根据每个学生的表现来打分。虽然我取得了不错的成绩，但我对我的团队成员并不熟悉。我不知道他们的兴趣及偏好，因为我只能在演讲前见他们几次（而已）。如果我能与他们合作，并一起讨论棘手的问题，我就可以了解他们并与他们建立友谊。

作　者：薛航

成绩单：

Your Scores from Test Date:
**February 27, 2023**

| Total<br>(0 – 120) | Reading<br>(0 – 30) | Listening<br>(0 – 30) | Speaking<br>(0 – 30) | Writing<br>(0 – 30) |
|---|---|---|---|---|
| 115 | 30 | 28 | 27 | 30 |

# Topic 11
## 该不该限制大学涨学费?

Section 1 of 1

Your professor is teaching a class on social science. Write a post responding to the professor's question.

**In your response, you should do the following.**
- Express and support your personal opinion.
- Make a contribution to the discussion in your own words.

An effective response will contain at least 100 words.

Professor

University tuition (money you pay to receive university education) in the United States more than doubled over the 20 years between 1990 and 2010. Tuition increases have caused students to take out more loans (debts) to be able to afford a university education. Some people argue that universities should not be able to increase tuition costs so much because it puts a burden on students when they have to pay off the loans. In your view, should universities be able to increase tuition as much as they wish, or should there be limits on tuition increases? Why?

00:09:59  Hide Timer

Stephen

I think college tuition should go up. Nowadays, the income of everyone in the society is higher. For example, the price of food is also higher. University operation also needs cost; tuition is an important source. If the tuition does not rise, it will affect the income of the university, so that the university will not have enough budget to improve the campus environment and teaching laboratory, hire professors and employees, and finally students will suffer losses.

Juan

I don't think college tuition should go up. Because everyone has the right to receive education, the government should guarantee the citizens the right. If some students are excellent, but can't afford the tuition, then they can't go to college. The society will eventually lose the talent. In addition, the government can subsidize universities through taxes and other means.

| Cut | Paste | Undo | Redo | Hide Word Count 0 |

##  审题 & 构思

这道题目属于比较新颖的政府类话题，涉及大学教育、大学学费和政府职责。对于同学们来说，既抽象又具体，因为大家似乎有大致的回答，但是如何展开分析和论述比较困难。可以在草稿纸上写下大致想法，切入点可以从减轻学生负担、教育质量、对国家的好处等方面形成直接—间接的递进过程，使得展开具有层次感。展开则要延续这种想法，顺藤摸瓜：学生负担为什么大了？对于哪些家庭来说负担大？教育的本质是什么？教育培养了什么样的有用人才？这些人才如何对社会做贡献？能形成有序论述即可。

## My answer 1

It is the incremental college tuitions and other fees that considerably aggregate students' financial burdens. To be more specific, one common take on the situation blames institutions of maintaining college expenses at a lower level for reducing the learning efficiency of the American students. This, however simply isn't the case. The truth is that government programs weren't prepared for the rise in education costs, and the federal grant programs began to shift to subsidized loan programs. With less subsidization from government sources, colleges turned elsewhere to pay for educations: tuition and fees owed by families. However, along with the inflation and relatively slow increases on average wages, the education portion occupies larger in the whole family incomes. Imagine the hard-working American parents who work eight or nine hours a day for six days a week cannot guarantee their children to receive college education from the state university, and who should be blamed? Or consider a son from a single mother has to drop out of the high school despite of his extraordinary all-A transcript but since his mother, maybe a janitor in a motel, tells that she cannot afford the tuition.[1] What a joke about our university! (197 words)

## My answer 2

The necessary constraints on college tuitions contribute to the educational equality. That is to say,[2] we have to clarify a simply but ignored fact for a long period of time: To be educated is the right for students, and to educate is the duty of the university. It is this fundamental law that now has been monetized and been turned into a money laundering scheme—an opportunity for tax collectors and investors to extort money from students and professionals alike. With this gradual trend, we oversee how important education today is to a country and to its people. It is the educated force, who creates all the difference, and not merely money—as without education and proper knowledge, development will lose its trail and money will become futile. With this regard, the educational system or our government, as its fundamental duty towards its citizen, should encourage university education, without burdening the students, especially the needy ones, with the liability of tuition fees to solidify the very purpose of education, the equal right to access the knowledge. (175 words)

[1] 举例论证：引发读者对于特定情境的想象：辛勤工作的家庭无法让孩子得到公立学校的教育机会，或者单亲家庭的孩子学术优异却被迫因为经济原因提前放弃学业，社会和大学将多悲剧。

[2] 解释主题句：学习是学生的权利，教育是大学的义务，不能让金钱腐蚀了教学这些神圣的机会，反而让投机者盆满钵满。

## My answer 3

I want to make my response to those stupid worries about lower efficiency caused by lower costs of college tuitions. Exempting the students from excessive tuition costs of university education will have manifold advantages. There will be an inevitable increase in the number of students opting for higher education—especially those with merits but not with enough funding.[3] This will provide the State a continuous stream of well professional engineers, doctors, theorists, artists, thinkers, writers and revolutionists, among the many. With sound education, these people can positively contribute towards the society — in fields of advancement of technology, health research, increase in aesthetic values, literary works, towards deeper understanding of the past and future, and bringing in changes. Students, thus can be encouraged to pursue higher education for positively contributing towards research and development, or academics. Hence, a nation stands to benefit, in all aspects, raising the potential of people and itself in general, thus welcoming a "smarter economy".
(158 words)

[3] 解释主题句：有了更低廉的教育成本，更多人接受教育后，学生会成为各行各业的高级人才：工程师、医生、科学家等。

### Words & Phrases

| | |
|---|---|
| incremental 递增的 | average wages 平均工资 |
| subsidized loan programs 补贴贷款计划 | transcript 成绩单 |
| inflation 通货膨胀 | extort from 向……勒索 |

Topic 11　该不该限制大学涨学费？　079

> 参考译文

Professor

从1990年到2010年的20年间，美国的大学学费（为接受大学教育而支付的钱）翻了一倍多。学费上涨导致学生们借更多的贷款来支付大学学费。一些人认为大学不应该增加这么多学费，因为这会给学生带来负担，毕竟他们必须偿还贷款。在你看来，大学是否可以随心所欲地增加学费，还是应该（出台举措）限制学费的增加？为什么？

Stephen

我认为大学学费应该上涨。如今，社会上每个人的收入都提高了。例如，食品的价格也更高了。大学的运作也需要成本，学费是一个重要来源。如果学费不上涨，就会影响大学的收入，使大学没有足够的预算来改善校园环境和教学实验室、聘请教授和员工，最后学生就会吃亏。

Juan

我认为大学学费不应该上涨。因为每个人都有接受教育的权利，所以政府应该保障公民的权利。如果有些学生很优秀，但付不起学费，那么他们就不能接受大学教育，社会最终会（因此）失去人才。此外，政府可以通过税收和其他方式补贴大学。

## ■ My answer 1

　　增加的大学学费和其他费用大大增加了学生的经济负担。更具体地说，对这种情况的一种普遍看法是，将大学费用维持在较低水平的院校，会降低美国学生的学习效率。然而，事实并非如此。事实上，政府的各类计划并未针对教育成本的上涨做好准备，（比如）联邦拨款计划开始转向补贴贷款计划。由于政府补贴减少，大学转向支付教育费用的其他渠道：来自于各个家庭的学费支出。然而，由于通货膨胀，还有平均工资增长相对缓慢，教育支出在整个家庭收入中所占的比重越来越大。想象一下，辛勤的美国家长们每周需要工作六天，每天需要工作八九个小时，居然不能保证（自己的）孩子可以（有足够的学费）接受州立大学的大学教育，又该怪谁呢？或者，想象一下，一个单身母亲的儿子尽管成绩非常出色，但不得不从高中辍学，而这只是因为他的母亲是一名汽车旅馆的看门人，实在负担不起孩子的学费。我们大学在开什么玩笑！

### ■ My answer 2

对大学学费的必要限制有助于教育公平。也就是说，我们必须澄清一个简单却长期被忽视的事实：受教育是学生的权利，教育是大学的职责。正是这条基本规则，（教育）现在已经被货币化并变成了洗钱计划——税收人员和投资者有机会从学生和专业人士那里勒索钱财。伴随着这种渐进的趋势，我们可以看到当今教育对一个国家及其人民的重要性。是这股受过教育的力量，而不仅仅是金钱，创造了我们所处社会的不同——如果没有教育和适当的知识，发展将失去踪迹，金钱将变得毫无意义。在这方面，教育系统或我们的政府，因其对公民担有基本的职责，应该鼓励大学教育。不应该给学生压力，特别是给有资金需求的学生增加学费的负担；应该以巩固教育的本源为目的，保障学生平等获取知识的权利。

### ■ My answer 3

我想对那些愚蠢地担忧因大学学费降低而导致（学习）效率降低的想法做出回应：免除学生过多的大学教育费用将带来多方面的好处。（如果是这样），选择接受高等教育的学生人数将不可避免地增加——尤其是那些成绩优异但资金不足的学生。这将为国家提供源源不断的优秀的、专业的工程师、医生、理论家、艺术家、思想家、作家和革命家等。通过良好的教育，这些人可以为社会做出积极贡献——在技术进步、健康研究、审美价值提升、文学作品等领域，加深对过去和未来的了解，并带来变革。因此，可以鼓励学生接受高等教育，为研发或学术做出积极贡献。因此，（通过教育）提高国民和自身的（学术）潜力，国家将在各个方面受益，从而（自信地）迎接"更智能的经济"。

作　者：薛航

成绩单：

Your Scores from Test Date:
**November 16, 2022**

| Total (0–120) | Reading (0–30) | Listening (0–30) | Speaking (0–30) | Writing (0–30) |
|---|---|---|---|---|
| **112** | **30** | **29** | **23** | **30** |

# Topic 12
## 年轻时出国旅游更好 or 老了以后出国旅游更好？

Section 1 of 1

Your professor is teaching a class on tourism. Write a post responding to the professor's question.

**In your response, you should do the following.**

- Express and support your personal opinion.
- Make a contribution to the discussion in your own words.

An effective response will contain at least 100 words.

Professor

Today we will have a discussion about traveling. While the recent COVID-19 crisis almost sets the tourism industry back in ten years, traveling remains the most sought-after activities for upcoming holidays. Were it not for travel restrictions, global tourism would have most likely continued to be on the rise. Interestingly, different age groups can experience different levels of satisfaction when traveling abroad. For you, is it better to travel abroad to visit different countries when you are younger than when you are older? Please give your opinion and let's start the talk.

Topic 12　年轻时出国旅游更好 or 老了以后出国旅游更好?

00:09:59　　Hide Timer

**Danika**

I think young people can gain more by traveling. Because the school pressure and work pressure are very big, modern young people are very tired. Besides, foreign countries have their own attractive cultural and tourist attractions. It is better for young people to go out to relax themselves and adjust their mood. In addition, traveling can also exercise their independence and self-confidence, because they need to deal with a lot of travel matters by themselves.

**Edgar**

I think it's better for people to travel when they're older. First of all, traveling needs to cost a lot of money. If young people can't afford it, they may have to ask their family to bear the cost or spend money in advance by credit card, which is unfair. When they are older, they will have a stable income to support themselves, so that they can decide where to travel, according to their own consumption level.

| Cut | Paste | Undo | Redo | Hide Word Count 0 |

### 审题 & 构思

此话题属于较为常见的外国旅行和选择相结合的题目。破拆题目只需要结合"外国旅行的内容""年龄群体的特点"两方面入手即可。需要注意的是，这里说的 young 和 old 并不一定指小孩子和退休的老人，只是一个相对的概念。很多同学一旦把 older 理解成老年人，行动缓慢，题目反而受到限制。展开外国旅行的话题尽量选择广为熟知的内容，如著名的国家公园，经典、人文地理的内容可以引入，使得自己的论述更具体和生动；同时可以及时地引入对比，突出自己的论点，也可以作为段落总结。

### My answer 1

A better-known benefit of traveling is that it offers a shift in perspective, which is exactly what younger people need to develop a more mature mindset. Most people spend their formative years in just one community, surrounded by neighbors from undifferentiated cultural backgrounds and of similar social status. The lack of contact with the outside world could result in the tendency to take things for granted and to develop tunnel vision, affecting young people's judgement and values. By going on a trip to other countries, young people get to see societies and lifestyles that are otherwise unimaginable. For example,[1] when children from wealthier countries, say, the US, set foot on Congo, the reality that some of the world's population still need to toil in sun-scorched fields from morning to dark, may permanently change their cognitive paradigm. Consequently, they may return home, feeling more blessed and content. All it takes is a few weeks from their summer vacation. Waiting until an older age to travel abroad, on the other hand, entails higher opportunity costs due to busy work schedule, and it is much harder to reconstruct one's way of thinking than when one is younger. (194 words)

[1] 举例论证：将国家具体化、细化一下描述，深入解释主题观点；并用 older age 做了反向论证。

Topic 12　年轻时出国旅游更好 or 老了以后出国旅游更好？

## My answer 2

The fact that younger tourists have a more ardent yearning for new experience makes their journeys more enjoyable. It has been scientifically proven that young people display a higher level of curiosity towards the unknown aspects of life. While people in their forties may take great pleasure in trying new restaurants or splurging on expenditures, those in their twenties, who are not yet accustomed to the unchanging daily routine, seek novelty as well as adventures. Being able to explore an unfamiliar country allows them to get away from day-to-day drudgery, kicking them out of their comfort zone and forcing them to discover other possibilities in life, ones that people may not pursue at an older age. A college student embarking on an adventure into the Amazon Jungle may be impressed by its biological diversity and thus switch his major. A fresh graduate enjoying his first attempt at scuba diving in Indonesia may be inspired to get his diving certificate.[2] The urge to explore a new territory wanes as people age because they subconsciously assume that they have seen it all and that there is less to expect in a trip. In this sense, young people's stronger curiosity sends them out to enthusiastically explore the world beyond their homeland. (208 words)

[2] 举例论证：细化前面的解释，采用多例法。大学生在亚马孙丛林中探险，在印度尼西亚尝试潜水。

**Words & Phrases**

| | |
|---|---|
| set back 使延误；耽误 | have a more ardent yearning for new experience 对新体验有更强烈的渴望 |
| sought-after 受欢迎的 | splurge on expenditures 挥霍 |
| undifferentiated 无差别的 | day-to-day drudgery 日常繁重无聊的工作 |
| take things for granted 自以为理所当然 | comfort zone 舒适区 |
| tunnel vision 视野狭窄；井底之蛙 | wane 减弱 |
| toil in sun-scorched fields from morning to dark 从早到晚在烈日炙烤的田野里劳作 | subconsciously 下意识地 |
| cognitive paradigm 认知模式 | |

> **参考译文**

**Professor**

今天我们来讨论一下旅游。虽然最近的COVID-19危机几乎使旅游业倒退了十年,但旅游仍然是即将到来的假期中最受欢迎的活动。如果没有旅行限制,全球旅游业很可能会继续增长。有趣的是,不同年龄段的人在出国旅游时体验到的满意度也不同。对你来说,在年轻的时候出国到不同的国家旅游,是否比在年老的时候去旅游更好?请发表你的意见,让我们开始讨论。

**Danika**

我认为年轻人可以通过旅行获得更多。因为(年轻人)在学校的压力或工作压力都很大,所以现代的年轻人都很累。此外,国外也有其吸引人的文化和旅游景点。因此,年轻人最好出去放松一下,调整一下心情。此外,旅行还可以锻炼年轻人的独立性和自信心,因为他们需要自己处理很多旅行事宜。

**Edgar**

我认为人们年纪大了再去旅游比较好。首先,旅行需要花费很多钱。如果年轻人(自己)负担不起,他们可能不得不让家人承担费用或通过信用卡提前花钱,这是不公平的。当他们长大后(再去旅游),他们会有一份稳定的收入来养活自己,这样他们就可以根据自己的消费水平来决定去哪里旅游。

## My answer 1

旅行的一个广为人知的好处是,它能改变视角,这正是年轻人成长过程中让自己的心态更成熟所需要的。大多数人只在一个社区里度过他们的成长期,周围都是来自相同的文化背景和相似社会地位的邻居。缺乏与外界的接触可能导致人们倾向于认为什么事情都是理所当然的,视野会变狭隘,这会影响年轻人的判断力和价值观。通过去其他国家旅行,年轻人可以看到原本无法想象的社会和生活方式。例如,当来自更富裕国家的孩子,比如美国,踏上刚果时,他们会亲眼看到世界上一些人口仍然需要

Topic 12　年轻时出国旅游更好 or 老了以后出国旅游更好？

从早到晚在太阳炙烤的田野里劳作。这一现实可能会永久地改变他们的认知方式。因此，当他们回到家时，会感到更幸福和满足，（而这一心态上的转变）只需要（占用）他们暑假中几周的时间。另一方面，由于（后续）繁忙的工作日程，如果等到岁数大一些再出国旅行，会存在更高的机会成本，而且重建自己的思维方式要比年轻时困难得多。

## ■ My answer 2

年轻的游客对新体验的渴望更加强烈，这会使得他们的旅行更加愉快。相关科学实验已经证明，年轻人会对生活的未知方面表现出更高的好奇心。40 多岁的人可能会非常喜欢尝试新餐馆或挥霍钱财，而 20 多岁的人还不习惯一成不变的日常生活，（他们更愿意）寻求新奇和冒险。能够探索一个陌生的国家，可以让他们摆脱日常的苦差事，让他们走出舒适区，发现生活中的其他可能性，这些是人们在年岁大一些以后可能不会再去追求的。一个进入亚马孙丛林去探险的大学生可能会对它的生物多样性印象深刻，继而可能会改变他的专业。一个在印尼享受第一次潜水的应届毕业生可能会受到启发，来获得他的潜水证书。随着年龄的增长，（人们）探索新领域的冲动会减弱，因为他们潜意识里会认为自己已经看过了许多，不会对旅行本身报以更多期望。从这个意义上说，年轻人更强烈的好奇心会使他们去热情地探索他们自己所在国家以外的（广阔）世界。

作　者：薛航

成绩单：

Your Scores from Test Date:
**November 2, 2022**

| Total<br>(0 – 120) | Reading<br>(0 – 30) | Listening<br>(0 – 30) | Speaking<br>(0 – 30) | Writing<br>(0 – 30) |
|---|---|---|---|---|
| 113 | 30 | 28 | 25 | 30 |

# Topic 13
## 该不该期望别人保持礼貌?

**Section 1 of 1**

Your professor is teaching a class on humanity. Write a post responding to the professor's question.

**In your response, you should do the following.**
- Express and support your personal opinion.
- Make a contribution to the discussion in your own words.

An effective response will contain at least 100 words.

Professor

Today we are talking about the politeness. While modern technology has enabled instantaneous communication and unprecedented convenience, it has also remarkably sped up our pace of life. As much as it promotes productivity, this hectic lifestyle comes with a few byproducts, one of which is the lack of politeness. "Because the world today is just so busy and crowded, we should not expect people to be polite to one another." Do you agree with this statement? Please give your opinion and let's start the talk.

00:09:59   Hide Timer

Aldrich

I think in many specific situations, people need to stand up for themselves; being polite to others will lead to a lot of problems. For example, I often meet people who are different from me in my work philosophy and attitude. If I am too polite to others, my boss may feel that I am not competent enough. In addition, if a person is always polite to others, then others will think that this person is easy to compromise, so there will be a lot of excessive demands.

Gary

I think people need to be polite to others. Because if one person is polite to others, there is a high probability that others will be polite to that person, and vice versa. So treat others the way you expect them to treat you. No one likes a rude or disrespectful person, so being polite to others equals being polite to yourself.

| Cut | Paste | Undo | Redo | Hide Word Count 0 |

## 审题 & 构思

此问题属于比较抽象的话题，是较难的题目，因为大部分同学对于题目理解没问题，但是难以展开合理的论述。思考的点可以基于日常生活、学习和职场，设定一个具体的场景，使得大家能明确礼貌和不礼貌分别是什么，那么话题就很好代入了。所以，需要从一开始就明确礼貌的形式、礼貌带来的好处，一旦明确了论述的终点，具体内容围绕这个终点展开即可。

## My answer 1

Politeness in modern times takes much simpler forms,[1] which means the effort to show respect to others is unlikely to disrupt one's tight schedule. Gone are the days when people greeted each other with firm handshakes or even giving a theatrical bow. Social etiquettes have certainly evolved over the years to a point where people find more manageable and more efficient ways to demonstrate how respectful you are towards a person or an organization.[2] For example, when engaging in a conversation with someone else, we should listen more attentively and refrain from the urge to make it all about us. When meeting a new client, we should dress professionally to denote a sense of importance. When making an appointment, we should make sure that we show up on time.[3] None of these trivial acts exploits our time, nor do they cost anything. The core of politeness has always been about being aware of and respecting the feelings of others rather than just going through the motions,[4] so it is wrong to assume that the necessity of politeness will wane as our pace of life speeds up. After all, even small gestures like saying please and thank you at Starbucks can be a signal of kindness and demeanor.[5] (207 words)

[1] 主题句：礼貌可以体现在比过去更简单的形式中。

[2] 解释主题句：和过去人们见面时的握手和鞠躬相比，现在人们体现礼仪的形式要更简洁了。

[3] 举例论证：三个生活中常见的例子，进一步解释观点。

[4] 解释例子：这些行为和动作并不费时费力；进一步阐述being polite的重点是尊重他人，而不是一些烦琐的动作。

[5] 再次用生活中的例子总结主体段。

Topic 13　该不该期望别人保持礼貌?

 My answer 2

It is the increasingly busy and crowded life we live nowadays that makes politeness an even more sought-after quality.⁶ Many studies revealed that city dwellers experience a significantly higher level of anxiety and stress than rural residents,⁷ and the main culprit is their tendency to optimize time management. In other words, it appears that people are trading happiness for higher productivity. Trying to be polite to one another, in this sense, helps to ease anxiety without slowing things down. This is especially true when it comes to daily encounters with strangers. Just imagine how it can ruin your mood if someone accidentally steps on your foot in the underground but walks away without saying sorry.⁸ The word "sorry" works magical because it implies an apologetic attitude in this case. The same holds true in the workplace, where impolite behavior, such as aggressiveness, can fuel the fire of a tense situation, making it difficult to resolve conflicts. In fact, the truth that we tend to be infuriated by rude and offensive manners reflects just how much we value politeness in modern life. (181 words)

**6** 主题句：正是因为现代生活的繁忙，让礼貌成了一种更受欢迎的品质。

**7** 解释主题句中提到的现象：现代社会繁忙、高压的生活。

**8** 举例论证：生活中常见的一个案例（不小心被别人踩到脚）进一步解释观点，论证礼貌的重要性。

| Words & Phrases | |
|---|---|
| instantaneous 立即的 | denote 表示，意指 |
| unprecedented 前所未有的 | sought-after 受欢迎的 |
| hectic 忙碌的 | culprit 罪魁祸首；引起问题的事物 |
| byproduct 附带的结果 | be infuriated by rude and offensive manners 被粗鲁无礼的举止激怒 |
| social etiquettes 社交礼仪 | |

Professor

我们今天聊聊礼貌问题。虽然现代科技给我们带来了即时通信和前所未有的（很多其他）便利，它也大大加快了我们的生活节奏。我们忙碌的生活方式虽然提高了工作效率，也带来了一些副产品，其中之一就是缺乏礼貌。"因为今天的世界是如此繁忙和拥挤，我们不应该期望人们对彼此有礼貌。"你是否同意这样的说法？请发表你的意见，让我们开始讨论。

Aldrich

我认为在很多特定的情况下，人们需要维护自己，对别人有礼貌会导致很多问题。例如，我经常遇到与我在工作理念和态度上不同的人，如果我对其他人太客气，我的老板可能会觉得我不够胜任。另外，如果一个人总是对别人彬彬有礼，那么别人会认为这个人很容易妥协，所以会有很多过分的要求。

Gary

我认为人们需要对别人有礼貌。因为如果一个人对其他人有礼貌，其他人很可能会对那个人也有礼貌，反之亦然。所以，你希望别人怎样对待你，你就怎样对待别人。没有人喜欢粗鲁无礼的人，所以对别人有礼貌等于对自己有礼貌。

■ My answer 1

在现代，礼貌的形式要简单得多，这意味着尊重他人并不需要给一个人紧张的日程安排带来任何干扰。过去人们通过互相握手，甚至夸张地鞠躬的方式表示礼貌的日子已经一去不复返了。多年来，社会礼仪已经发展，人们找到了更易于管理、更有效的方法来展示你对一个人或一个组织的尊重。例如，当我们和别人交谈时，我们应该更仔细地倾听，避免让话题的核心都围绕着自己。见到新客户时，我们应该着装正式以表重视。做了预约，我们应该确保准时到达。这些琐碎的行为都没有花费我们太多时间，也没有让我们付出任何代价。礼貌的核心一直是意识到和尊重他人的感受，而不仅仅是表现在行动中，所以认为礼貌的必要性会随着我们生活节奏的加快而减弱是错误的。毕竟，在星巴克，即使是像说"请"和"谢谢"这样的行为，也可以被视作善良和风度的信号。

## My answer 2

正是因为我们现在的生活越来越忙碌，礼貌成了一种更受欢迎的品质。许多研究表明，城市居民的焦虑和压力水平明显高于农村居民，其罪魁祸首是他们优化时间管理的倾向。换句话说，人们似乎是在用幸福来换取更高的生产力。从这个意义上说，对彼此保持礼貌，有助于缓解人们的焦虑，同时不会让效率降低。当涉及每天与陌生人的接触时，尤其如此。想象一下，如果在地铁里有人不小心踩到你的脚，但没有说对不起就走开了，这会严重破坏你的心情。"对不起"这个词很神奇，因为在这种情况下，它暗示了一种道歉的态度。同样的情况也适用于工作场所，一些不礼貌的行为，比如（一个人）表现出对同事的攻击性，会加剧紧张局势，使冲突难以解决。事实上，我们往往会被粗鲁和无礼的举止所激怒，这一事实反映了我们在现代生活中是多么（需要）重视礼貌。

作　者：薛航

成绩单：

Your Scores from Test Date:
**September 25, 2022**

| Total<br>(0-120) | Reading<br>(0-30) | Listening<br>(0-30) | Speaking<br>(0-30) | Writing<br>(0-30) |
|---|---|---|---|---|
| 109 | 30 | 26 | 23 | 30 |

# Topic 14
## 暑假上课 or 参观博物馆?

Section 1 of 1

Your professor is teaching a class on education. Write a post responding to the professor's question.

**In your response, you should do the following.**
- Express and support your personal opinion.
- Make a contribution to the discussion in your own words.

An effective response will contain at least 100 words.

Professor

In today's class we'll have a discussion about the summer session. The summer break is not only a long-established tradition cherished by the educational system but is beneficial for the well-being of teenagers. Recently, a high school plans to impose a new requirement for students in the eleventh grade, who can either choose to spend a few weeks studying the university subjects they favor in advance, or pay visits to local museums and study historical relics. Which one of these two options do you think would be most beneficial for students, and why?

00:09:59   Hide Timer

Patton

Having a preview of college courses before you enroll helps a lot. College is more difficult, and by taking college courses, such as science courses, you can understand how scientific laws are generated and deduced, and courses about liberal arts can give you more chances to elevate reading and writing skills. In addition, if you prepare college content in advance, it will be easier to study when you enter college because you are already familiar with the content.

Nicole

I think it would be more interesting to visit a history museum. Students are already under a lot of pressure to study and do homework every day, so some outdoor activities can help them really de-stress. Besides, there are all kinds of interesting exhibits in the museum, which students can observe closely. This kind of experience cannot be obtained from reading books.

| Cut | Paste | Undo | Redo |   Hide Word Count  0

**审题 & 构思**

这是一道比较常见的教育类话题，但是需要注意题目对于群体（11 年级）和时间段（暑假）有明确的限定，所以在展开过程中应该照顾到这些限定条件。常见的错误就是脱离这些限定条件，自说自话，导致论述跑题。提前准备和亲身经历都是比较容易想到的观点，展开过程中还需要引入具体内容和场景，就会使得有话可说，不会出现词穷的情况，所以平时对于不同学科内容和描述需要留心记忆。一旦能形成完整的表述，那么类似的例子就可以作为储备的语料，在 Academic Writing 题目中也可以稍加修改呈现。

 **My answer 1**

I agree with Patton and I want to add that students can get a head start with earlier exposure to their interested field of study if they choose to study college level courses during summer session.[1] For one thing, learning college courses in advance can help students better adapt to university life. There are striking differences between high school and university, and such differences are not restricted to course content. The learning objectives and teaching methods that high school students take granted for are largely inapplicable in higher education. Therefore, preparing well in advance and studying university courses in summer vacation by the end of high school can help students smooth the transition to college life in the future. Grasping some rudiments of their future major lays a solid foundation for academic success in their freshman year.[2] No matter which discipline students plan to pursue in college, the saying that "a good start is half done" holds true. With a preliminary understanding of a field, students are more likely to master a subject faster, which not only impresses

[1] 观点：学生们可以早些接触自己感兴趣的学术领域。

[2] 观点补充：提前为大一学习铺垫基础。

the professor but also bolsters self-confidence in their learning ability. Going on a trip to museums and historical sites, on the other hand, is not necessarily helpful since local history and culture probably do not matter that much in college, when students tend to move to other cities for getting a degree. (230 words)

## My answer 2

In my opinion, studying the university subjects they favor in advance provides an opportunity for students to determine whether they are genuinely fond of the subject they choose.[3] College courses cover a much wider range of disciplines than high school curriculum,[4] and it is hard to tell what to expect merely from their names. One needs to attend lectures and study a few chapters before he can confirm how enthusiastic he is about the subject. By taking major-related courses, these soon-to-be freshmen avoid making a mistake in major selection. For example, many teenagers think of the study of Astronomy as an exploration into the vast space, assuming that it mainly deals with the strange and mysterious facets of the universe. While black holes and constellations sound fascinating, astronomical studies are primarily based on mathematic models and physics that have everything to do with numbers and formulas. It is not until teenagers are exposed to Astronomy courses will they realize the stark contrast between their imagination and reality.[5] In this sense, taking a course that lasts only several weeks offers a trial experience for students ready to apply for an ideal university, but museums and historical sites, which will not make a difference to their future, seem secondary.[6] (207 words)

[3] 主题句：学生们可以借此机会知道自己是否真的对自己选择的领域感兴趣。

[4] 阐述大学专业和课程的特点：很难从名字去了解具体的学习内容和方向。

[5] 举例论证：用"天文学"一个具体的专业做例子，给出具体的细节，描述丰富的例子（黑洞、星座、数学模型、物理等），阐述学生们的想象和学科的本质往往有很大的出入。

[6] 总结论点，并且再次指出另一个选择的不足之处。

## Words & Phrases

| | |
|---|---|
| get a head start 抢占先机 | a good start is half done 良好的开端是成功的一半 |
| inapplicable 不适用的 | soon-to-be 即将成为……的 |
| rudiment 基础；基本原理（或技能） | facet 方面；（事物的）部分 |
| discipline 学科 | constellation 星座 |

### 参考译文

Professor

在今天的课上，我们将讨论一下夏季课程。暑假不仅是教育系统一直以来重视的一项悠久传统，同时也对青少年的健康有诸多益处。最近，一所高中计划对11年级的学生实施一项新要求，即他们可以选择花几周时间提前学习自己喜欢的大学课程，也可以选择参观当地的博物馆和研究历史文物。你认为这两种选择哪一种对学生更有利，为什么？

Patton

（我认为）在入学前预习一下大学课程将会很有帮助。大学课程难度会更大，而且通过（学习）大学课程，比如理科课程，你可以了解科学定律是如何产生和推导的，（学习）文科课程可以给你更多的机会提高阅读和写作技能。另外，如果提前准备好大学的内容，进入大学后学习起来会更容易，因为你已经对内容很熟悉了。

Nicole

我觉得去历史博物馆会更有趣。学生们每天都承受着很大的学习和做作业的压力，所以一些户外活动可以帮助他们真正减压。此外，博物馆里有各种有趣的展品，学生可以近距离观察，这种亲身体验是无法从书本中获得的。

### My answer 1

我同意Patton的观点，我想补充说的是，学生们选择在暑假学习大学课程，提前接触到他们感兴趣的学习领域。一方面，提前学习大学课程可以帮助学生更好地适应大学生活。因为高中和大学（知识）之间存在显著的差异，而且这种差异并不仅限于课程内容。高中生所适应的学习目标和教学方法在很大程度上并不适用于高等教育。于是，提前做好准备，在高中结束的暑假学习大学课程，可以帮助学生顺利向未来的大学生活过渡。另一方面，掌握未来专业的一些基础知识会为大学一年级的学业成功奠定坚实的基础。因为无论学生打算在大学里学习什么专业,"好的开始是成功的一半"的说法都是正确的。通过对一个领域的初步了解,学生更有可能更快地掌握一门学科,这不仅会给教授留下深刻印象,而且也会增强他们学习的自信心。事情的另一面,(我认为暑期)去博物馆和历史遗迹旅行并不一定会对学生有什么帮助,因为当地的历史和文化在大学里可能并不那么重要,尤其是当学生们搬到其他城市上大学的话。

## My answer 2

我认为预先学习他们喜欢的大学内容会为学生们提供一个机会,来确定他们是否真的喜欢他们所选择的科目。大学课程将会比高中课程涵盖更广泛的学科,仅仅从课程的名字很难预测具体内容是什么。一个人需要(真正)上课和学习(一个课程)几章的内容,才能确认他对这个学科有多少热情。通过参加与专业相关的课程,这些即将入学的新生可以避免在专业选择上犯错误。例如,许多青少年认为天文学的研究是对广阔宇宙的探索,认为它主要探究宇宙中奇怪而神秘的方面。虽然黑洞和星座听起来很吸引人,但天文研究主要是基于数学模型和物理学,是需要跟数字和公式打交道的。直到青少年接触到天文学课程,他们才能意识到他们的想象和现实之间的鲜明对比。从这个意义上说,花费几周时间参加一门课程,会为准备申请理想大学的学生提供一种试用体验,但(暑期去参观)博物馆和历史遗迹好像是次要的,对他们的未来并不会有什么(正面的)影响。

作 者:薛航

成绩单:

Your Scores from Test Date:
**July 09, 2022**

| Total<br>(0 – 120) | Reading<br>(0 – 30) | Listening<br>(0 – 30) | Speaking<br>(0 – 30) | Writing<br>(0 – 30) |
|---|---|---|---|---|
| 112 | 29 | 27 | 26 | 30 |

# Topic 15
# 放任朋友犯错比伤害友情好?

Section 1 of 1

Your professor is teaching a class on humanity. Write a post responding to the professor's question.

In your response, you should do the following.
- Express and support your personal opinion.
- Make a contribution to the discussion in your own words.

An effective response will contain at least 100 words.

Professor

Today we will have a discussion about the friendship. Friends are an enhancing part of life. They provide companion, comfort as well as camaraderie to get us through ups and downs. But occasionally, friends can demonstrate poor judgment and make mistakes unknowingly. A prevailing saying goes that letting a friend make a mistake is better than saying or doing something that would destroy the friendship. What is your remark on this saying?

00:09:59  Hide Timer

**Anthony**

I think it is better to keep silent when a friend makes a mistake, so that he or she can learn a lesson from it. For example, if your friend does not review and listen to the teacher carefully, then when he or she encounters subject-related problems, you need to let him or her summarize by himself or herself instead of helping him or her in the wrong but straightforward way. So, he or she can truly reflect on his or her behavior and make changes.

**Zane**

I think the most important thing in friendship is to help. So when a friend makes a mistake, in fact, most of the time he or she does not realize the mistake. In this case, you need to tell him or her immediately. Then he or she will stop the mistake and avoid further damage.

Cut  Paste  Undo  Redo                    Hide Word Count  0

## 审题 & 构思

此题目属于比较抽象的话题，难以展开。破解的关键点在于对于友谊进行思考和分析：友谊能给人们带来什么影响，展开的内容同样需要有非常具体的例子，因为友谊和犯错属于非常具体的定义。但同时也会非常抽象，读者也许能明白友谊，但是大家恐怕不了解何种友谊，什么场景下的友谊，什么人之间的友谊。这就会使得犯错误这种后续描述空洞无意义，所以引入考试作弊和朋友进行投资建议的例子，具体化叙述会更好写。

## My answer 1

True friends help each other grow as a person. A good friend will always give you honest opinions and will prefer constructive criticism over destructive, which not only leaves your confidence in tact but also forces you to correct your mistakes. This is a strong advantage of having a friend around as we grow and mature as a responsible adult. For example, some students would collaborate to cheat in exams for higher scores. These students must be friends that they can trust to begin with, and they even trust each other enough to a point where they scheme for better grades. But a true friend will not indulge this kind of wrongful behavior.[1] Instead of passing the answer to the friend, one should be able to point out that cheating in exams is unfair and strictly prohibited by the honor code, warning him or her of the dire consequence of getting caught. It is likely that a friend with integrity will take the warning and change his or her mind, which helps him or her learn the lesson of integrity. Therefore, there is every

[1] 举例论证：用考试作弊这个事例做论证去进一步细致地解释论点，真正的朋友不会同流合污，而是会警示你走上正轨。

reason to believe correcting a friend's mistake is doing him or her a favor rather than harming his or her feelings. (201 words)

 My answer 2

Remaining silent can cause regrets for our friends.[2] Telling the truth is critical in dealing with friendships, especially when our friends are heading towards a wrong direction. While we were still students, the mistakes we made were mostly insignificant, like being disrespectful to teachers, being rebellious, or telling little lies. These are misconducts that would do little to affect our future.[3] But as our roles shift from being a student to being a parent, a worker and a taxpayer, our decisions weigh heavily on our future. Imagine that if a friend of yours decides to run a fancy restaurant in your neighborhood and considers it profitable, you know it is a mistake because most people in your neighborhood prefer cooking on their own, who do not eat out frequently. At this time, if you choose to refrain from telling him or her that it will fail, your friend will suffer great loss by this investment, and he or she will even blame you for not being helpful. In this sense, silence is detrimental to friendships. (175 words)

[2] 亮明观点：面对朋友的错误保持沉默，有可能会让朋友留下遗憾。

[3] 举例论证：朋友在工作上的错误决策，你及时指出，会帮助他避免巨大的经济损失。

| Words & Phrases | |
|---|---|
| camaraderie 友情 | honor code 诚信守则 |
| tact（处事、言谈等的）老练；得体 | integrity 诚实正直 |
| indulge 放纵；听任 | |

参考译文

Professor

今天我们会讨论友谊的话题。朋友是生活中有益的一部分：他们提供陪伴、安慰和友情，使我们度过风风雨雨。但偶尔，朋友也会表现出判断力差的问题，在不知不觉中犯错误。有一种说法是，让朋友犯错比说或做一些会破坏友谊的事情要好。你怎么看这个问题？

Anthony

我认为当朋友犯错时最好保持沉默，这样他或她就能从中吸取教训。例如，如果你的朋友没有认真复习和听老师讲课，那么当他或她遇到知识点相关的问题时，你需要让他/她自己总结，而不是以错误却直接的方式帮助他/她。这样，他/她才能真正反思自己的行为并做出改变。

Zane

我认为友谊中最重要的是互相帮助。所以当一个朋友犯了错误，事实上，大多数情况下，他/她都没有意识到这个错误；在这种情况下，你需要立即告诉他/她。这样，他/她会停止错误，及时止损。

### My answer 1

真正的朋友会互相帮助对方成长。一个好朋友总是会给你诚实的意见，更喜欢建设性的批评而不是破坏性的，这不仅让你保持自信，也迫使你纠正你的错误。在我们成长为一个负责任的成年人的过程中，有这样的朋友会是（我们成长路上）一个强大的优势。例如，一些学生会合作在考试中作弊以获得高分。这些学生必须是一开始就可以互相信任的朋友，而且他们彼此信任的程度足够深，以至于他们可以共同做此获高分的计划。但一个真正的朋友不会纵容这种错误的行为。一个人不应该把答案告诉朋友，而应该指出考试作弊是不公平的，这是诚信守则严令禁止的；应该警告他/她作弊被抓住的可怕后果。一个正直的朋友很可能会接受这个警告并改变主意，这也能帮助他/她吸取教训。因此，我们有充分的理由相信，纠正朋友的错误是帮他/她一个忙，而不是伤害他/她的感情。

 **My answer 2**

　　保持沉默可能会给我们的朋友们带来遗憾。(我认为)说出真相在处理友谊时至关重要，尤其是当我们的朋友正走向一个错误的方向时。当我们还是学生的时候，我们所犯的错误大多都是微不足道的，比如不尊重老师、叛逆或者说些小谎。这些不当行为对我们的未来影响不大。但随着我们的角色从学生转变为家长、上班族和纳税人的时候，我们的决定就会严重影响我们的未来。想象一下，假设你的一个朋友决定在你的社区开一家高档餐厅，并认为它有利可图。你从一开始就知道这是一个错误，因为你社区里的大多数人更喜欢自己做饭，他们不经常出去吃饭。在这个时候，如果你选择不告诉他/她这个项目会失败，你的朋友将会因为这个投资而遭受巨大的损失，他/她甚至日后会责怪你没有提供相应的有效意见。从这个意义上说，沉默对友谊其实是有害的。

作　者：薛航
成绩单：

Your Scores from Test Date:
**June 26, 2022**

| Total<br>(0-120) | Reading<br>(0-30) | Listening<br>(0-30) | Speaking<br>(0-30) | Writing<br>(0-30) |
|---|---|---|---|---|
| **108** | **30** | **25** | **23** | **30** |

# Topic 16
# 儿童进行小组活动比独自活动好？

**Section 1 of 1**

Your professor is teaching a class on pedagogy. Write a post responding to the professor's question.

**In your response, you should do the following.**
- Express and support your personal opinion.
- Make a contribution to the discussion in your own words.

An effective response will contain at least 100 words.

Professor

In today's class, we're going to talk about reforming the way children are taught. Teachers have abandoned the individual-oriented learning approach, adopting a strategy that encourages group discussions and teamwork. Many schools for young children require students to work together in small groups instead of working alone for many of their learning activities. What's your opinion?

**Venus**

I think it is very important for children to study independently. In the process of learning, because everyone's capability, learning pace and attitude are different, they can find out what they don't know and write it down, and then ask the teacher for help. If students were organized to study in a group, some contents will be ignored and missed if other members know it, but one particular student doesn't actually understand. In addition, it is more efficient to study alone. Children can focus on the content without thinking about chatting with other group members. Especially for children with weak self-discipline, this is better.

**Jason**

I think group study is better for children. During group discussions, children can observe how outstanding team members take notes, analyze problems and summarize key points. Many learning abilities and methods that are not covered by teachers in class are directly observed by children. In addition, we also need to consider that because of the teacher as an adult, the content of the teaching may not be understood by the children. But children communicate better with each other, so it's easier for them to collaborate and solve problems.

## 审题 & 构思

这道题目不难，属于比较常见的小组合作或者个体单干的选择题目，但是需要注意题目有明确的限定条件：小学生群体。所以，分析展开后续内容要特别注意代入相应年龄群体的特质，否则会被判定跑题。观点从社交技能或者协作者的角度出发分别进行叙述（具体论述在两篇范文里）。在论述过程中只需要引入相应的例子就可以呈现具体的内容，同时符合题目对年龄群体的限制。

## My answer 1

I think group work fosters social skills. Social skills are often tied to many facets of adulthood, but socialization starts as early as when we are toddlers. When young children are organized into small groups to accomplish a common goal that the teacher announces, they inevitably initiate conversations and exchange flows of ideas. Even an introvert is willing to speak out his unique perspective on a subject matter in group discussion since it appears to be the only way to make contributions. For example, when a group of four young children are told to draw a painting depicting the view of spring, they may start by brainstorming the images that represent spring, and then they carefully examine each option, persuading others or making compromises when necessary.[1] Although these are not deliberate efforts to socialize, when they immerse themselves in group work, they unconsciously develop the ability to understand the needs and feeling of others, which is critical as they grow to be socially connected members in society. Individual work, on the other hand, isolates young children and impedes human interaction. As much as it promotes independent thinking, it suppresses children's

[1] 举例说明：四人小组完成绘画、头脑风暴、核查选项，必要时做出妥协。

nature to interact with others in their formative years. This certainly makes it less worthy than cooperative learning. (208 words)

 **My answer 2**

In my opinion, children get to learn from a young age how to be a good team player. Being able to work as part of a team is crucial for academic success as well as career advancement. In today's knowledge economy, only with the ability to cooperate can one's efforts and expertise become visible to others. In primary education, therefore, teachers should encourage students to explore a subject matter and work out a solution in small groups, which requires teachers to assume more of a facilitative role than a direct instructional one. Consider writing class; the teacher can divide the class into several groups and make them create a short story using the characters they just read about in a novel. In ten minutes, each group member will take on different roles and be assigned particular tasks to help finish the story. The one with most creativity may be in charge of writing the plots while the one adept at writing may polish and proofread the work.² Over time, young children will learn about how to contribute their best abilities to fulfill a common goal in teamwork. (187 words)

**2** 举例论证：老师在教学中应该多鼓励学生完成小组活动和协作任务，找到自己的定位，完成自己的任务，实现集体的目标。

| Words & Phrases | |
|---|---|
| facet 方面；（事物的）部分 | introvert 内向的人 |
| toddler 蹒跚学步的孩子 | expertise 专业知识 |

参考译文

Professor

今天的课上，我们要谈谈改革孩子们教育方式的问题。教师们放弃了以个人为导向的学习方法，采用了一种鼓励小组讨论和团队合作的策略。许多幼儿学校要求学生在小组中一起学习，而不是单独学习。你怎么看这一举措？

Venus

我认为孩子独立学习是很重要的。在学习的过程中，由于每个人的能力、学习速度和态度都不一样，孩子们可以先找出自己不懂的知识并记下来，然后向老师寻求帮助。如果学生被安排在一个小组中学习，一些学习内容如果其他成员已经知道了，就会被理所当然地忽略和遗漏，而这个学生其实却并没有真正理解。此外，独立学习的效率会更高。孩子们可以专注于内容，而不用考虑与其他小组成员聊天。特别是对于自律性较弱的孩子，这样的学习方式更好。

Jason

我认为小组学习对孩子们更好。在小组讨论中，孩子们可以观察到优秀的团队成员是如何记笔记、分析问题和总结要点的。很多老师在课堂上没有讲到的学习能力和方法，孩子们都能直接观察到。此外，我们还需要考虑到，由于教师是成年人，教学的内容可能不会被孩子们轻易理解。而孩子们（同龄人）之间更好交流，会更容易促进合作和解决问题。

### My answer 1

　　我认为小组学习可以培养社交技能。社交技能通常与成年后的许多方面有关，但社交早在我们蹒跚学步的时候就开始了。当小孩子被分成小组来实现老师布置的共同目标时，他们不可避免地会开始对话和交流想法。即使是一个内向的人也愿意在小组讨论中说出自己对一个主题的独特观点，因为这似乎是做出贡献的唯一途径。具体来说，当四个孩子分到一组，被告知画一幅描绘春天景色的画时，他们可能会先头脑风暴代表春天的图片，然后仔细检查每个选择的正确性，说服其他人或在必要时做出妥协。虽然这些都不是刻意的社交，但当他们沉浸在团队工作中时，他们无意识地发展了理解他人需求和感受的能力，这在他们成长为相互关联的社会成员的过程中，是至关重要的（一种能力）。另一方面，独立学习会使孩子变孤立，阻碍人际互动。它虽然促进了独立思考，但也抑制了孩子在成长时期与他人互动的天性。这必然使它不如合作学习更值得推崇。

## My answer 2

我的观点是，孩子们从很小的时候就应该开始学习如何成为一名优秀的团队协作者。能够作为团队的一员来工作，对学术成就和职业发展都至关重要。在当今的知识经济中，只有有了合作的能力，一个人的努力和专业知识才能被其他人看到。因此，在小学教育中，教师应该鼓励学生分组探索一个主题，并制订解决方案；这要求教师承担的角色更多是课堂促进作用，而不是直接的传授教学作用。我们以写作课为例：教师可以把班级分成几组，让他们用刚在小说中读到的人物来创作一个短故事。在十分钟内，每个小组成员将承担不同的角色，并被分配特定的任务来帮助完成整篇故事。最有创造力的人可能会负责写情节，而擅长写作的人可能会润色和校对作品。随着时间的推移，孩子们将学习到如何贡献他们最好的能力，来实现团队合作的共同目标。

作　者：薛航

成绩单：

Your Scores from Test Date:
**November 01, 2022**

| Total<br>(0–120) | Reading<br>(0–30) | Listening<br>(0–30) | Speaking<br>(0–30) | Writing<br>(0–30) |
|---|---|---|---|---|
| 110 | 30 | 28 | 22 | 30 |

# Topic 17
# 面对问题应该轻松 or 严肃?

Section 1 of 1

Your professor is teaching a class on social science. Write a post responding to the professor's question.

**In your response, you should do the following.**
- Express and support your personal opinion.
- Make a contribution to the discussion in your own words.

An effective response will contain at least 100 words.

Professor

Life can sometimes be tough with all kinds of problems, and none of us is exempted. It is controversial about what attitude we should take in the face of issues or crises. Some people support to try to figure out a solution to the problems in a light-hearted manner, while others consider that a serious attitude towards problems, even a minor one, is necessary. Which approach do you prefer? Why?

00:09:59   Hide Timer

Candice

I think we need to be serious when facing problems. Through serious attitude, we can be clear to complete the details of the task, to clarify the requirements of each link, even to avoid the mistakes made by others. Because many tasks are not easy to complete, if a detail is wrong, it is likely to waste time and energy in the end. In addition, being serious is also a good attitude to study and work. If one notices that he/she has this quality, then he or she will be more assured to undertake important tasks in the future. In other words, there will be more opportunities.

Sagan

I think it is better to take a relaxed attitude towards problems. For example, when we do certain work or school tasks, an employee or a student has this characteristic. When they get along with others, the atmosphere does not become too oppressive. People in depressed environments tend to play badly, or when people think too much, it can lead to failure in the end. In addition, people with such a personality in the group can liven up the atmosphere in the group, so that everyone will not be too nervous, but also will be harmonious.

| Cut | Paste | Undo | Redo | Hide Word Count | 0 |

## 审题 & 构思

这道题目提问非常抽象，也就是大家能明确题目是什么，理解上没有障碍，但是感觉论述无从下手，解决这样问题的关键就在于要大胆引入例证和细节，代入到相应场景中。

## My answer 1

While facing obstacles, serious attitudes can help us overcome setbacks, leading us to better improve ourselves. As old Chinese saying goes, do not commit an evil act just because it is small in scale, highlighting the attitude of strictness and seriousness.

For example, with the popularity of bike-sharing, the problem of bike damage has emerged in an endless stream, and children are the main saboteurs. In the eyes of some parents, children destroying bike sharing is just a kind of mischievous behavior, so they just deal with this problem with light blame. However, they ignore the fact that the reason why a problem has become a universal one is that no one takes it seriously. If everyone regards breaking a shared bike as an issue with the same gravity of breaking the law, it could not have become a ubiquitous issue.[1] It is just like if parents see their children commit murder or steal, they will surely stop it seriously because normal parents do not want their children to break the law, even if there is a law on the protection of minors. (183 words)

[1] 举例论证：父母纵容孩子对共享单车做一些小破坏，如果每个人都这么做，那么带来的破坏是巨大的。

## My answer 2

Serious attitudes while dealing with problems will take us to success. For individuals,[2] if a child is habitually absent-

[2] 以个人为例，父母帮助孩子克服精力不集中的问题，严肃认真对待，养成良好的习惯。

minded and his parents feel that the problem seriously affects the future of the child, they will place greater emphasis on it and not indulge the child to continually make mistakes so as to cultivate good habits for the child. For enterprises,³ if a company considers laxity as severe damage to the company's interests, there will not be so many employees who fail to fulfill their duty. All big problems arise from the lack of serious attitudes, and all general problems are derived from the failure to solve smaller problems. For society as a whole, if people of all professions and social statuses always adopt a laugh-it-off attitude towards problems, industries and sectors that are otherwise thriving will be stagnant. This is because excessively optimistic people tend to turn a blind eye to trivial problems. (153 words)

**3** 分类论证：以企业为例，公司严肃纠正员工的工作态度。

| Words & Phrases | |
|---|---|
| overcome setbacks 克服挫折 | habitually absent-minded 习惯性走神 |
| Do not commit an evil act just because it is small in scale. 勿以恶小而为之。 | place greater emphasis on 更加重视 |
| saboteur 破坏者 | laugh-it-off 一笑置之 |
| mischievous behavior 恶作剧行为 | |

参考译文

Professor

生活有时会很艰难，时刻充斥着各种各样的问题，没有人能幸免。面对问题或危机，我们应该采取什么样的态度，仁者见仁，智者见智。一些人支持以轻松愉快的态度寻找解决问题的办法，而另一些人则认为对待问题需报以严肃的态度，即使是很小的问题。你更喜欢哪种处理问题的方法？为什么？

**Candice**

我认为处理问题的态度应该严肃一些。投入严肃认真的态度（处理问题），我们可以明确完成任务的细节，澄清每个环节的要求，甚至避免别人可能会犯的错误。由于很多任务完成起来很不易，如果一个细节出错，很可能最终既浪费了时间又消耗了精力。此外，严肃认真也是一种良好的学习和工作态度。如果一个人有意去锻炼自己的这种品质，那么他/她将更有信心在未来承担重要的任务。换句话说，会有更多的机会。

**Sagan**

我觉得处理问题时持轻松的态度会更好。例如，当我们做某些工作或学校任务时，有员工或学生具有这种特征。那么他们与人相处时，气氛不会变得过于压抑。处于抑郁环境中的人，往往会表现得很糟糕，或者当人们想得太多时，最终会导致失败。另外，在小组里有这样性格的人，可以活跃小组气氛，大家不会太过紧张，也能融洽相处。

### ■ My answer 1

在面对障碍时，严肃的态度可以帮助我们克服挫折，引导我们更好地提高自己。正如中国老话所说，勿以恶小而为之，凸显了严格和严肃的态度。以我们身边的事情举例，随着共享单车的普及，自行车损坏的问题不断发生，这其中孩子是主要的破坏者。在一些父母看来，孩子破坏共享单车只是一种淘气的行为，所以他们只是用不痛不痒的指责来处理这个问题。然而，他们忽略了这样一个事实，即一个问题之所以会普遍存在，是因为没有人会认真对待它。如果每个人都认为破坏一辆共享单车是一个严重的问题，是违法的，它就不可能成为一个无处不在的现象。就像如果父母看到他们的孩子谋杀或偷窃，他们肯定会认真地阻止，因为正常的父母不希望他们的孩子违反法律，即使有保护未成年人的法律存在。

### ■ My answer 2

在处理问题时的严肃态度将使我们走向成功。对于个人来说，如果一个孩子习惯性地心不在焉，而他的父母觉得这个问题严重影响了孩子的未来，他们就会更加重视它，自然不会纵容孩子不断犯错，这会为孩子培养一个好的习惯。对于企业来说，如果一个公司认为松懈会严重损害公司利益，就自然不会有那么多的员工不履行职责。所有的大问题都来源于缺乏严肃的处理态度，而所有的一般问题都来自于未能解决的更小的问题。对整个社会来说，如果每一个行业和社会地位的人总是对问题采取一种一笑置之的态度，那些蓬勃发展的行业和部门注定将会停滞不前。这是因为过于乐观的人往往会对一些琐碎的问题视而不见。

作　者：薛航

成绩单：

Your Scores from Test Date:
**October 03, 2022**

| Total<br>(0 – 120) | Reading<br>(0 – 30) | Listening<br>(0 – 30) | Speaking<br>(0 – 30) | Writing<br>(0 – 30) |
| --- | --- | --- | --- | --- |
| 112 | 29 | 27 | 26 | 30 |

# Topic 18
# 政府花钱探索太空是不是浪费钱?

Section 1 of 1

Your professor is teaching a class on political science. Write a post responding to the professor's question.

**In your response, you should do the following.**
- Express and support your personal opinion.
- Make a contribution to the discussion in your own words.

An effective response will contain at least 100 words.

Professor

Humans have always looked up into the night sky and dreamed about space. In the latter half of the 20th century, rockets were developed that were powerful enough to overcome the force of gravity to reach orbital velocities, paving the way for space exploration to become a reality. Some, on the contrary, are concerned and argue that it is a waste of money to launch space projects since there could be better practical usage on our planet. What's your opinion?

Topic 18　政府花钱探索太空是不是浪费钱？

00:09:59　　Hide Timer

William

I think space exploration is very necessary because it is of great significance to human society. For example, in space exploration, advanced computers are used to measure spacecraft trajectory and core control, which is something that no company can accomplish. Many other key manufacturing processes, materials and even medicine will be developed in the space environment. All these will definitely benefit the whole human society.

Young

I think space exploration will waste a lot of precious resources. Because human's understanding of the universe is still very limited, many mysteries are not clear to us; that is to say, in the process of space exploration, we will certainly encounter failures and various dangers which will cause tremendous loss to the money allocated on this space project. So the money spent on building spaceships, investing in space equipment and training astronauts should be spent on things that actually help people, like health care and education.

| Cut | Paste | Undo | Redo | | Hide Word Count 0 |

## 审题 & 构思

这是一道经典的政府类话题，所以破题的依据应该联想到政府的任务和职责。另外，题目提到了非常有意思的太空探索，也就是前沿科技题材，所以可选取的撰写角度非常多。具体地说，可以从政府的责任、发展经济和太空探索的直接后果、科技突破等角度展开论述。在具体展开的过程中，依然要通过引入具体的例子来增加说服力，比如说明 GPS 的应用对于就业、新兴行业发展的促进和推动作用，都是很具体和熟悉的例子。文章中变色的地方，是一些固定表达，建议同学们平日留心记忆。

## My answer 1

William is right for it is the government funding on the space projects that massively leads to the technological breakthrough.[1] That is to say, the exploration in the universe required the edge-cutting technologies to ensure the safety of astronauts and spaceships. The processors of central administrative system, wireless sensors and other electronic algorithm are of complexity and perplexity. They are prohibitively expensive for relevant theory-drafting, designing, experiments and manufacturing processes, and therefore no single corporation as well as the organization can ever afford. If given sufficient financial supports from the governmental level, the technological difficulties might be conquered by scientists and engineers, therefore developing them into mature enough for civil usage and practice. For example, the GPS developers probably did not foresee how this technology would transform almost every industry, as well as day-to-day life, on a global scale. Using maps and travel atlases and stopping to ask for directions are now largely anachronisms. GPS has enabled ride-hailing services, as well as package tracking

[1] 这段内容中标注粗体的文字较多。坦白讲，考生们肯定认为这篇范文可以理解，但很难模仿。中间的具体表达，是我本人长期以来的语料积累，而非考场上限时情况下的即兴表达。在新 TOEFL 的背景下，不足 10 分钟的学术写作，更需要考生们在考场上调取自己脑子里的一些语料，这就需要平日的积累，而不是等待考试时"现想"。

and delivery. It has improved our fitness by tracking our workouts and our safety by quickly providing our location in emergency situations. GPS will be there in the future to facilitate emerging technologies such as self-driving cars and package deliveries by drones. (206 words)

## My answer 2

An evident reason to champion governmental funds on space travel and exploration involves economic gains. More than fifty years of human activity in space have produced societal benefits that improve the quality of life on Earth.[2] The first satellites, designed to study the space environment and test initial capabilities in Earth orbit, contributed critical knowledge and capabilities for developing satellite telecommunications, global positioning, and advances in weather forecasting. We have witnessed that many newly emerged positions that never ever existed in the past continue to boom in the contemporary society, which is tightly related with universe programs. In other words, space exploration initiated the economic development of space that today, year after year, delivers high returns for invested funds in space. Likewise, the market and even the entertainment industry, films and movies, many of them are storied and originated from space travel and exploration. Audience loves to watch and is willing to pay for them. It is hard to imagine what the life would have become if there were missing funds that may financially drive the program specialized at universe. (180 words)

**[2]** 举例论证：卫星对于地球上人们生活的帮助。

## Words & Phrases

| | |
|---|---|
| overcome the force of gravity to reach orbital velocities 克服重力以达到轨道运行速度 | corporation 公司 |
| technological breakthrough 技术突破 | travel atlases 旅行图册 |
| edge-cutting 前沿的 | anachronism 不合时宜 |
| wireless sensors 无线传感器 | ride-hailing services 打车服务 |
| electronic algorithm 电子算法 | package tracking and delivery 包裹追踪和投递 |
| complexity 复杂性 | satellite telecommunications 卫星通信 |
| perplexity 难以理解的事物 | global positioning 全球定位 |
| prohibitively expensive 贵得令人望而却步 | |

### 参考译文

**Professor**

人类一直仰望夜空，梦想着太空。20 世纪下半叶，人类研制出了强大到足以克服重力达到轨道运行速度的火箭，为太空探索成为现实铺平了道路。相反，一些人担心并认为，发展太空项目是浪费钱，因为在我们的星球上这些钱可以有更好的实际用途。你怎么看这个问题？

**William**

我认为太空探索是非常必要的，因为它对人类社会意义重大。例如，在太空探索中，先进的计算机被用来测量航天器的轨道和核心控制，这是任何公司都无法做到的。许多其他关键的制造工艺、材料甚至药物都将在太空环境中进行研发，这些都可以最终使整个人类群体获益。

**Young**

我认为太空探索会浪费很多宝贵的资源。因为人类对宇宙的认识还很有限，很多奥秘我们还不清楚；这意味着，在太空探索的过程中，我们肯定会遭受失败和各种危险，这无疑会给发展太空项目的资金带来巨大的损失。因此，花在建造宇宙飞船、投资太空设备和培训宇航员上的钱应该花在真正帮助人们的事情上，比如医疗保健和教育。

### ■ My answer 1

William 说得没错，正是政府对太空项目的资金投入大大促进了技术突破。具体来说，人类对宇宙的探索，是需要使用尖端技术来确保宇航员和宇宙飞船的安全的。中

Topic 18　政府花钱探索太空是不是浪费钱？

央管理系统、无线传感器、其他电子算法是非常复杂的。相关的理论起草、设计、实验和整个制造过程，都非常昂贵，因此没有一家公司和组织能负担得起。如果政府给予足够的财政支持，科学家和工程师可能会克服技术困难，从而使其发展成足够成熟的技术，用于民用和实践。例如，GPS 开发人员可能没有预见到这项技术将如何改变全球范围内几乎所有行业以及人们的日常生活。现在使用地图和旅行图册，以及停下来问路都过时了。GPS 已经实现了叫车服务，以及包裹跟踪和递送功能。它甚至可以检测我们的身体状况，帮助我们更加健康；它还可以在紧急情况下定位我们，以保障我们的安全。GPS 将在未来进一步促进像自动驾驶汽车和无人机投送包裹等新兴技术的发展。

## My answer 2

　　我支持政府在太空旅行和探索方面投入资金的一个明显原因是出于经济收益方面的考虑。50 多年的人类太空活动产生了很多社会效益，提高了地球上（人们）的生活质量。第一批卫星旨在研究空间环境和测试地球轨道上的初始能力，为发展卫星通信、全球定位和天气预报方面的进展提供了关键的知识和能力。我们已经目睹，许多过去从未存在过的新领域在当代社会继续繁荣，这与宇宙计划紧密相关。换句话说，太空探索开启了太空相关的经济发展，现在年复一年，为太空投资资金带来了高回报。同样地，在市场甚至娱乐产业中，比如纪录片或影片（行业），其中许多故事都起源于太空旅行和探索。观众喜欢观看，也愿意为它们付费。很难想象，如果在推动宇宙探索的项目上缺少资金投入，我们的生活会变成什么样子。

作　者：薛航

成绩单：

Your Scores from Test Date:
**October 17, 2022**

| Total<br>(0–120) | Reading<br>(0–30) | Listening<br>(0–30) | Speaking<br>(0–30) | Writing<br>(0–30) |
|---|---|---|---|---|
| 111 | 29 | 30 | 22 | 30 |

# Topic 19
## 追随本心 or 遵守传统社会规则?

Section 1 of 1

Your professor is teaching a class on social science. Write a post responding to the professor's question.

**In your response, you should do the following.**
- Express and support your personal opinion.
- Make a contribution to the discussion in your own words.

An effective response will contain at least 100 words.

Professor

In our next week's discussion, we will focus on talking about your preference on following your own heart or following traditional society rules. Let's get prepared for this thought-provoking topic by exchanging ideas about your opinion. What is your thought?

00:09:59   Hide Timer

Jeremy

Many traditional rules in society were formulated earlier and are no longer applicable to the development of today's society. For example, few boys participated in synchronized swimming in the past, but as a male student, I was deeply attracted by synchronized swimming. I fashioned this club in my university and attracted many students who had the same interests as me. So I think we should firmly follow our own heart.

Laura

I think we should still follow traditional rules of society, because the existence of corresponding rules must have its reason. Follow one's own heart will make one appear different. However, following traditional rules of society will make one integrate into more groups, make more friends, and have more recognition.

| Cut | Paste | Undo | Redo | Hide Word Count 0 |

## 审题 & 构思

教授在引导学生讨论。这道题是一道二选一的题目，相对而言，选择遵循传统社会规则会比选择遵循个人本心更容易下笔。考场上为了凑足至少 100 词，需要拆开进行论述。作者选择从个人角度和社会角度去切入，遵循传统规则的好处是什么，受制于考场时间的限制，只论述理由，不展开具体事例的细节，同时在句子结构上进行必要雕琢，达到考试时拿到 5 分评分标准的目的。

## My answer 1

I think following the traditional rules of society is the better choice as it means taking fewer risks under different conditions,[1] which is better for the development of both individuals and communities, from the macroscopic perspective.

[1] 抛出自己的论点：遵循传统意味着我们会承担较小的风险。

The traditional rules that exist in our lives have all been practiced by thousands of generations before being taught to us.[2] Therefore, they are more likely to represent the most authoritative and feasible rules that would promote things developed in positive directions.

[2] 进一步解释遵循传统为什么意味着风险较小。

For individuals, if a teenager chooses to follow the traditional rules and laws, go to school on time and fulfil his/her time with academic readings and practice, there will be no way that the person loses precious opportunities to receive progressive suggestions from teachers.[3]

[3] 从青少年（个人）的角度进行论证，强调了上学（遵循传统规则）的重要性。

Also, society's development cannot be excluded from well obeying traditional rules.[4] When all members in the same community do the right things that satisfy the basic rules, such as going up stairs along the right-side walls, keeping quiet in the public library, or even producing environmentally-friendly products and abiding government

[4] 从社会宏观的角度论证为什么要遵守规则，而不能随心所欲。

regulations,⁵ the community would develop in positive directions instead of progressing backwardly. (184 words)

**5** 并列句的使用, 罗列原因。增加了句子的复杂程度和整篇文章句子的多样性。

 **My answer 2**

From my perspective, following the traditional rules allows people to accomplish their goals in a shorter period while maximizing their efficiency.⁶ There is no denying that the choice of following one's heart provides people with more opportunities and possibilities to do the things they want. However, insisting on one's own opinion can be time-wasting under some conditions because of the immature experience and the untested thinking.⁷

From personal perspective, when a young man follows his/her heart of chasing high aspirations and starting up a new business with lacking professional knowledge, his/her goals would be hard to achieve.⁸

From social perspective, when the government choose to invest lots of money in secondary industries instead of building infrastructure during the initial stage, extra time would be wasted because of lacking the useful infrastructures that should be built first. Also, the government cannot gain as much revenue as they imagine because they don't follow the traditional rule of laying the foundation before developing profitable industries.⁹

Therefore, following one's heart without considering the realistic problems that have already been concluded in traditional society's rules would slow down the working efficiency of both individuals and communities.¹⁰ (191 words)

**6** 抛出论点: 遵守传统规则能让人们更有效率地达到自己的目标。

**7** 段内进行让步, 适当承认遵从内心的好处, 让自己的论证更加客观、全面, 也更能融入讨论氛围。

**8** 从个人角度论证自己的理由, 受制于真实考试的时间限制, 不展开更多例子进行解释。

**9** 作者花了更多笔墨从宏观角度进行分析, 列举了政府投资的例子, 更多细节也在这一部分体现。

**10** 段落总结, 重述自己的论点。

## Words & Phrases

from the macroscopic perspective 从宏观上看　　initial 最初的

abide 遵守　　revenue 税收

**参考译文**

Professor: 在我们下周的讨论中,我们将重点讨论你更喜欢遵从自己的内心还是遵循传统的社会规则。让我们通过交流你的观点,来为这个发人深省的话题做好准备。你的想法是什么?

Jeremy: 社会上的很多传统规则都是较早时候制定的,已经不适用于当今社会的发展。例如,以往很少有男生参加花样游泳运动,但我作为男生就被花样游泳这项运动深深吸引。我在大学内创建了这个社团,吸引了很多和我有同样兴趣的同学。所以我认为我们应该坚定地遵循自己的内心。

Laura: 我认为我们还是应该遵循社会的传统规则,因为对应规则的存在肯定有它存在的道理。一个人遵循自己的内心会显得比较另类,而遵循社会传统规则会使自己融入更多群体,交到更多的朋友,获得更多的认同。

### ■ My answer 1

我认为遵循传统的社会规则是更好的选择,因为这意味着在不同条件下承担较少的风险,从宏观上看,这对个人和集体的发展都更好。

这些存在于我们生活中的传统规则在传授给我们之前,已经过了数千代人的实践,因此,它们更有可能代表最权威和最可行的规则,能帮助事情朝着积极的方向发展。

对个人来讲,如果一个青少年选择遵循传统的规则,按时上学,并通过阅读和社会实践来充实他/她的时间,那么这个人就不会失去从老师那里得到进步的建议的宝贵机会。

此外,社会的发展也不能无视传统规则。当同一社区的所有成员都按照基本规则做正确的事情时,例如靠右上楼梯,在公共图书馆保持安静,生产环保产品和遵守法规,那么社会就会朝着积极的方向发展,而不是倒退。

## My answer 2

我的观点是，遵循传统规则能使人们在更短的时间内实现目标，同时最大限度地提高效率。不可否认，选择追随自己的内心能使人们有更多机会和可能性去做自己想做的事。然而，由于不成熟的经验和未经论证的想法，在某些情况下，坚持自己的观点可能会浪费时间。

从个人的角度来讲，当一个年轻人选择听从自己内心的声音，追求远大抱负，在缺乏专业知识的情况下创业，他/她的目标将很难实现。

从社会的角度来讲，在社会发展的初始阶段，如果政府决定在第二产业投入大量资金而不是建设基础设施，将会因为缺乏应该先建设好的有用的基础设施而浪费额外的时间。同时，政府也会因为他们没有遵循在发展盈利行业之前奠定良好基础的规则而无法获得丰富的收入。

因此，跟随自己的内心，不重视传统社会规则中已经论证的现实问题，会导致个人和集体工作效率低下。

作　者：杨丰璐
成绩单：

Your Scores from Test Date:
**October 04, 2021**

| Total (0–120) | Reading (0–30) | Listening (0–30) | Speaking (0–30) | Writing (0–30) |
|---|---|---|---|---|
| 103 | 29 | 21 | 23 | 30 |

 **MyBest™ Scores** as of December 15, 2021
Your highest section scores from all valid test dates are shown below.

| Sum of Highest Section Scores (0–120) | Reading (0–30) | Listening (0–30) | Speaking (0–30) | Writing (0–30) |
|---|---|---|---|---|
| 109 | 29<br>Test Date: Oct 04, 2021 | 27<br>Test Date: Nov 14, 2021 | 23<br>Test Date: Dec 12, 2021 | 30<br>Test Date: Oct 40, 2021 |

# Topic 20
## 教师收入是否应该和学生的成绩挂钩？

Section 1 of 1

Your professor is teaching a class on social science. Write a post responding to the professor's question.

In your response, you should do the following.
- Express and support your personal opinion.
- Make a contribution to the discussion in your own words.

An effective response will contain at least 100 words.

Professor

There have been some on-going hot discussions on high-school teachers' salary and some argue that teachers should receive bonus if their students do well in exams since they must have put in effort educating their students. In your opinion, should teachers be paid according to how well their students perform in exams?

Topic 20 教师收入是否应该和学生的成绩挂钩? 131

00:09:59  Hide Timer

Fiona

I can hardly agree with this statement. In this case, teachers will treat each student differently. Students who perform well in exams can get more attention and praises from the teacher since they help the teacher earn extra payment. On the contrary, students who get lower grades in exams may be criticized harshly by the teacher no matter how much effort they've put into their study.

Phillip

I actually think that's a good idea. On one hand, teachers will be more motivated since money is involved. They will polish their teaching style and care more about their students' well-beings. On the other hand, it would be good for the school's reputation if students' overall performance improved.

| Cut | Paste | Undo | Redo | Hide Word Count 0 |

### 审题 & 构思

这是一道典型的 agree or disagree 的题目：老师的工资是否应该和学生的成绩挂钩。看到题目的时候，我首先做的事情是简单做一个思维导图。题目中的很多词都可以拿出来单独分析，比如"老师"和"学生"，可以分别讨论这个政策对于这两类人群的影响。再比如"how well their students perform"，这引发出对于一个老师教学质量评价的标准，这个标准不仅仅是学生的成绩，还应该有多方面的考量。

Fiona 持反方观点：不同意。Fiona 认为这种政策下，老师们会区别对待学生。读者可以顺着这个思路继续扩充下去，也可以对这个观点进行反驳，例如：老师们不一定会对学生们区别对待，反而会一视同仁，鼓励和帮助学生们提高成绩。

Phillip 持正方观点：同意。这个政策对于老师来说是个教学的动力，并且有助于提升学校的声誉。这个观点没有进行详细的解释和例证展开，读者可以在此基础上进行延展。

### My answer 1

I don't think that's a good idea.[1] Firstly, it's absolutely not fair to teachers if they are simply being judged by the performance of their students.[2] Things can go wrong during exams. Even a straight-A student will miss a blank or make mistakes and lose some points from now and then.[3] This is definitely not the fault of their teachers, and thus teachers should not be blamed and punished.[4] Second of all, it's unfair to students, too.[5] With such policy carried out, all the teacher will do is to make the students cram for exams and stuff them up with piles of exercise papers. They may not spend time polishing the slides or picking out a better teaching aid to make the class more efficient. Students won't get proper education in this case.[6] (133 words)

[1] 开头直接亮出自己的观点。

[2] 观点一：对于老师来说不公平。

[3] 进一步进行解释：好学生并不一定可以在考试中发挥得好，总有意外发生。

[4] 如果没有这句话，文章打分为 4 分；如果加上这句话，文章打分为 5 分。逻辑上要讲清楚，说到点子上，学生的表现会对教师产生什么影响，这是这个讨论话题的宗旨。

[5] 观点二：对于学生来说不公平。

[6] 进一步进行解释：老师的教学重心可能会跑偏，从而让学生们无法得到适当的教育。

### My answer 2

In my opinion, teachers should be paid according to

how well their students perform in exams.⁶ I strongly agree with Phillip's idea that such policy will act as a great motivation for teachers. I'd add that since students take exams regularly, it's the easiest and fairest way to evaluate how well a teacher handles the class.⁷

Fiona raised the point that teachers may criticize those students who don't do well in exams and I can hardly agree. In order to increase the income, the teachers will focus more on students with lower grades and help them to improve.⁸ For example, the teachers may stay after school and tutor those students, as well as assign study partners to them. (118 words)

**6** 开头亮出自己的观点。

**7** 认同 Phillip 的观点，但从另外一个角度进行补充：这也是最简单、最公平的评测方法了。

**8** 反驳 Fiona 的观点：我不认为老师会批评那些考得不好的学生，反而会花更多的时间去帮助他们提高。

| Words & Phrases | |
|---|---|
| straight-A student 全优生 | polish the slides 打磨幻灯片 |
| miss a blank 错过一个空 | assign study partners to... 分配学习伙伴 |
| cram for exams and stuff them up with piles of exercise papers 为考试死记硬背而且用成堆的练习试卷进行填鸭式学习 | |

## 参考译文

Professor

关于高中教师的工资问题，一直有一些激烈的讨论。有些人认为，如果学生在考试中表现出色，教师应该获得奖金，因为他们肯定努力教育了学生。在你看来，教师的工资应该根据学生在考试中的表现来支付吗？

Fiona

我很难同意这种说法。在这种情况下，教师会以不同的方式对待每个学生。在考试中表现出色的学生可以得到教师更多的关注和赞扬，因为他们可以帮助教师赚取额外的报酬。相反，那些在考试中成绩较差的学生可能会受到教师的严厉批评，无论他们在学习上付出了多少努力。

Phillip

事实上，我认为这是个好主意。一方面，由于涉及金钱，教师会更有动力。他们将完善自己的教学风格，更加关心学生的情况。另一方面，如果学生的整体表现有所提高，对学校的声誉也有好处。

### My answer 1

我认为这不是一个好主意。首先，仅仅根据学生的表现来评判教师是绝对不公平的。考试期间可能会出现差错。即使全优学生也会漏答一个空或犯些错误，时不时地丢一些分数。这显然不是教师的错误，因此教师不应该受到责备甚至惩罚。其次，这对学生也不公平。有了这样的政策，教师所要做的就是让学生们为考试死记硬背而且用成堆的练习试卷进行填鸭式学习。他们可能不会花时间打磨幻灯片或挑选更好的教学辅助工具来提高课堂效率。在这种情况下，学生将得不到适当的教育。

### My answer 2

在我看来，教师应该根据学生在考试中的表现来获得报酬。我非常同意 Phillip 的观点，即这样的政策将成为教师的巨大动力。我想补充一点，由于学生定期参加考试，这是评估教师教学的最简单、最公平的方法。

Fiona 提出，教师可能会批评那些考试成绩不好的学生，我很难同意。为了增加收入，教师将会更多地关注低分学生，并帮助他们提高。例如，教师可能会在放学后留下来辅导那些学生，并为他们分配学习伙伴。

作　者：刘静灏

成绩单：

Your Scores from Test Date:
**November 30, 2022**

| Total (0–120) | Reading (0–30) | Listening (0–30) | Speaking (0–30) | Writing (0–30) |
| --- | --- | --- | --- | --- |
| 117 | 30 | 28 | 29 | 30 |

# Part 3
# 新版托福学术写作话题范文

这部分遴选历年托福独立写作的高频题目，根据题材进行清晰的分类，包括教育类、生活类、社会类、工作类和政府类。共 25 篇高分范文，均已改编为改革后 Academic Writing 的样子。

# TOEFL
## 教 育 类

# Topic 1
# 老师要不要每天留作业？

Section 1 of 1

Your professor is teaching a class on education. Write a post responding to the professor's question.

**In your response, you should do the following.**
- Express and support your personal opinion.
- Make a contribution to the discussion in your own words.

An effective response will contain at least 100 words.

Professor

Homework has long been used as a teaching method. Now people are questioning this opinion. Some people think that the daily homework will increase the burden of students. At the same time, others believe that homework can promote students' learning effect. What is your take?

Topic 1　老师要不要每天留作业？

00:09:59　 Hide Timer

Alan

I insist that teachers are supposed to give homework every day, because repetition learning, such as homework, can help students reinforce what they have learned in class. Because of homework, students spend specific time every day reviewing, practicing what they have learned, thereby strengthening their mastery of knowledge with better learning results.

Vicky

I think daily homework will increase students' unnecessary burden. Take myself as an example, when I was young, I spent a lot of time finishing my homework every day, which made me nearly lose all the time to relax. So I just muddled through my homework, didn't learn much, and felt under a lot of academic pressure.

| Cut | Paste | Undo | Redo | Hide Word Count 0 |

### 审题 & 构思

Professor 抛出问题，即对比每天留作业的优劣性。Alan 强调重复性学习的优越性。Vicky 表明了不同观点，以自身为例子，说明每天留作业，学生可能会应付作业，还会丧失休息时间。

### My answer

I think it is a good idea for teachers to assign homework for the students to do every day. [1]

One good reason to do homework assignments every day is that kids will make time to study for a steady amount of daily homework. [2] It ensures that kids get into the habit of allotting time to get their work done. [3] This skill is essential for all aspects of life, especially for later employment. The student learns to focus on the task at hand and complete it before moving on to other activities, just as he or she will have to do in a career. [4]

Also, repetition is the best way to remember new concepts. [5] Many studies have shown that students learn better when they are exposed to an idea several times over the course of a few days rather than learning in one lump. [6] Therefore, a teacher can enhance the teaching results by having the students review several times as homework later. The homework ensures that the students remember the essential parts. [7]

Daily homework assignments teach kids to study regularly and reinforce important points. Therefore, I feel that teachers should assign homework every day. [8] (193 words)

[1] 主题句：教师每天布置作业是有益的。

[2] 论点一：每天做作业，有助于学生分配时间进行学习。

[3] 观点解析：详细说明做作业会让学生懂得分配时间学习。

[4] 论点延伸：每日完成作业本身对学生未来的工作也有正面影响，借此作者再次强调了每日布置作业的合理性。

[5] 论点二：重复性学习有利于学生掌握新知识。

[6] 引用论证：阐释重复性学习相较于一次性学习，更有利于学生掌握知识。

[7] 解释说明：借助此句，作者强调每天做作业的益处，从而进一步加强论点。

[8] 结尾：收束全篇，总结两个论点，强调主论点。

Topic 1　老师要不要每天留作业？

## Words & Phrases

| | |
|---|---|
| allot time 分配时间 | learn in one lump 单次学习 |
| task at hand 手头的任务 | reinforce important points 加强重点 |
| repetition 重复 | |

### 参考译文

Professor
作业一直被用作一种教学手段。如今人们对于这一教学手段产生了疑问。有的人认为，每天的作业会增加学生负担。与此同时，也有人认为作业能够巩固学生的学习效果。你怎么看？

Alan
我倾向于老师应该每天留作业，因为作业等重复性学习的方式能够帮助学生巩固在课堂上学习到的知识。有了作业（这种形式），学生每天会花特定时间重温、练习自己学过的内容，由此加强对知识的掌握，从而取得更好的学习效果。

Vicky
我认为每天留作业会给学生增加不必要的负担。以我自身为例，我小时候每天都花很多时间完成作业，这让我失去了几乎所有放松的时间。因此，我（那时）只是随便应付作业，那样既没有学到更多知识，又感觉学业压力很大。

### My answer

我认为老师每天给学生布置作业是一个好主意。

每天做家庭作业的一个好的理由是，学生会腾出固定的时间完成作业。（老师）每天留作业会让学生养成分配时间来完成工作的习惯。这项技能对以后生活的各个方面都很重要，尤其是对以后的工作有意义。如同在职场中一样，学生要学会专注于手头的任务，并在进行下一项任务之前完成它。

而且，重复学习是记忆新知识的最好方法。许多研究表明，学生在几天的时间里多次接触一个知识，相较于一次性学习，他们的学习效果更好。因此，老师可以通过家庭作业，让学生在作业中多次复习所学内容，从而加强教学成果。家庭作业可以让学生记住学习的重点。

每天的家庭作业（可以）教会孩子们有规律地学习，巩固重点。因此，我觉得老师应该每天布置作业。

# Topic 2
# 自己帮同学 or 建议同学问老师?

Section 1 of 1

Your professor is teaching a class on education. Write a post responding to the professor's question.

**In your response, you should do the following.**
- Express and support your personal opinion.
- Make a contribution to the discussion in your own words.

An effective response will contain at least 100 words.

Professor

Peers' help is common. Should it be suggested that peers help each other academically? Suppose one of your classmates needs help with some schoolwork. You have good knowledge on the subject. Do you suggest your classmate to ask you for help or to find a professional tutor for help? Why?

00:09:59  Hide Timer

Adam

I think I will help my classmates myself. It will give me great satisfaction to help my classmates. As a student, I can better understand students' confusion about the subject. At the same time, with similar knowledge background, it is easier for me to explain knowledge to students, so that classmates can achieve better learning results. So I would offer help to my classmates personally, which is good for both of us.

Belle

I think students should find a professional tutor. As a more knowledgeable teacher, she/he is better able to identify problems in students' learning and provide them with more professional help. Peers often can only solve those superficial problems; they can not make up for the loopholes in students' learning. Therefore, I would advise students to seek professional help.

| Cut | Paste | Undo | Redo | Hide Word Count 0 |

## 审题 & 构思

根据题目，需要选择更容易提供论据的观点。就这道题而言，我认为前者更容易提供论点论据，即帮助他人可以让自己获得内心的满足感，并让同学获益。Adam 给出观点，因为亲自帮助同学可以让双方获益，所以应该亲自提供帮助。Belle 强调导师的专业性，认为应该寻求专业帮助。

## My answer

If one of my classmates needed help with a subject I know well, I would offer to assist.[1] First, I would feel good because I like doing generous deeds. If I am able to solve a friend's problem, I will feel like I have made the world a better place in a small way.[2] Also, I am not the only person who benefits from helping a classmate, though.[3] My classmate can save a lot of money without paying a private tutor to explain those confused questions. Besides, I know my classmate well, so I can use analogies that make sense to my classmate.[4] For instance, if a friend who plays basketball is having problems with percentages in math class, I can use examples related to percentages of baskets made versus shots missed. Knowing my friend's interests helps me make the explanation more applicable to everyday life than an abstract explanation from a professional tutor.[5]

Helping a classmate with schoolwork is beneficial for both the classmate and myself. Therefore, I would suggest that the classmate come to me for help with a subject I know well.[6] (185 words)

[1] 主题句：作者认为应该自己帮助同学。

[2] 论点一：阐明帮助同学能让自己获得内心的满足感。

[3] 论点二："我"为同学讲解，对同学大有帮助。

[4] 论点展开："我"能帮助同学省下家教费用而且还能用同学理解的方式教学。

[5] 举例说明："我"能够用同学更接受的方式教学，优于专业导师，对同学更有帮助。

[6] 总结论点论据，收束全篇。

### Words & Phrases

| | |
|---|---|
| generous deeds 慷慨的行为 | private tutor 家教 |
| benefit from 从……受益 | analogy 类比 |

参考译文

Professor

同龄人之间的互相帮助十分常见。那么在学术方面，是否应该推崇同龄互助？假设你的一个同学在某科目的作业上有些疑问，你恰好很擅长这个科目，你会建议同学找你寻求帮助，还是建议他/她去找一位专业的导师呢？为什么？

Adam

我想我会亲自帮助我的同学。能够帮助同学，会让我非常有满足感。作为学生，我更能理解学生对这一学科的困惑。与此同时，因为我和同学拥有相似的知识背景，所以我为同学进行讲解更容易，这样同学会达到更好的学习效果。因此我亲自帮助同学，对我们双方都有好处。

Belle

我认为应该让同学找一位更加专业的导师。作为学识更加渊博的老师，她/他会更能发现学生学习中的问题，从而为学生提供更专业的帮助。而同龄人往往只能解决浅显的问题，不能弥补学生学习上的漏洞。因此，我更建议同学寻求专业帮助。

## My answer

如果我的一个同学在我擅长的科目上需要帮助，我会主动提供帮助。首先，我会因为我喜欢做好事而感到满足。如果我能解决朋友的问题，我认为我就可以以一种小小的方式让世界变得更美好。另外，我并不是唯一一个从帮助同学中受益的人。（与此同时，）我的同学可以节省资金，而不用花钱请家教来解释那些令人困惑的问题。此外，我很了解我的同学，所以我可以用类比的办法来解释给我的同学听。例如，如果一个打篮球的朋友在数学课上对百分比有困惑，我可以用投篮命中率和投篮不中的百分比来举例。了解朋友的兴趣可以使得我的解释更适用于日常生活，而专业导师的解释往往会很抽象。

帮助同学做功课对同学和我都是有益的。因此，我会建议同学在我擅长的科目上来寻求我的帮助。

# Topic 3
# 高中教师最重要的能力是什么？

Section 1 of 1

Your professor is teaching a class on teachers' qualities. Write a post responding to the professor's question.

In your response, you should do the following.
- Express and support your personal opinion.
- Make a contribution to the discussion in your own words.

An effective response will contain at least 100 words.

Professor

It is common sense that teachers need to be qualified. For high school teachers, they should possess many abilities, such as the ability to give students advice to plan for their future, the ability to find which students need help and provide them with help or the ability to encourage students to learn on themselves outside of the classroom, etc. Which ability do you think is the most important one for high school teachers? Why?

00:09:59   Hide Timer

Ben

I think it is most important for students to learn on themselves outside of the classroom, because this is a compulsory course for every young adult. At this age, students are about to become adults. Besides knowledge, they also need to learn to face the social life, and solving their own problems outside school is a kind of practice. So I think the most important thing for teachers is to teach students to solve problems outside of school.

Coco

I think the most important thing for teachers is to give students advice to plan for their future, especially for 15–18-year olds. At this stage, students begin to think about their future and especially need teachers' guidance. Take me for example, when I was in high school, I hoped to be a teacher in the future. My teacher gave me relevant advice and guidance, and now I have realized my dream of being a teacher.

| Cut | Paste | Undo | Redo | Hide Word Count 0 |

## 审题 & 构思

针对这道题，脑子里不妨想象一下自己最熟悉的一两位老师的形象，他们属于具有哪一类能力的老师，看能否对号入座，这样在稍后扩展创作的时候，容易刻画。Ben 提出观点，认为教会学生在校外解决问题最为重要。Coco 认为，为学生规划未来是教师最重要的能力。

## My answer

There are two basic ways to teach someone: Show the person what to do, and teach the person to solve problems by themselves.[1] I believe a good high school teacher uses the latter method so students can function well outside the school environment.[2] High school students are on the verge of becoming adults, and they need to be ready to face the new tasks in front of them. Teachers can help prepare students by teaching them to solve problems by themselves.[3] Granted, it is easier to give students a list of answers to memorize and make them pass a test, but that method is not effective outside of the school environment. There is no one to give simple answers to life problems. Students need to understand the process of evaluating pros and cons in cases to come up with a decision when there is no correct answer.[4] A good teacher prepares the students by not only explaining answers to questions, but showing the reasoning process that gets to the best answer. High school teachers should avoid just having students memorize answers. Students need to learn the process of solving problems so they are prepared for adult life.[5] (197 words)

[1] 交代理论背景，探讨两种教学方法。

[2] 主题句：作者认为，对于高中生，最重要的是让他们能在课堂外解决自己的问题。

[3] 主题句展开：交代高中生的特点，以及对教师的要求。

[4] 观点解析：学生要面对的是更加复杂的社会生活。

[5] 收束全文，结束全篇。

Topic 3　高中教师最重要的能力是什么？　　149

| Words & Phrases | |
|---|---|
| on the verge of 即将 | evaluate pros and cons 评估利弊 |
| be ready to 准备好 | show the reasoning process that gets to the best answer 展示得出最佳答案的推理过程 |

参考译文

Professor

众所周知，教师需要称职。对于高中教师来讲，他们需要具备很多能力，比如：给学生建议规划未来的能力，发现哪些学生需要帮助并为他们提供帮助的能力，鼓励学生在课堂外自学的能力等。你认为对高中教师来讲，什么能力最重要？为什么？

Ben

我认为学生学会在课外自学是最重要的，因为这是每一个年轻人的必修课。在这个年龄段，学生们即将成为成年人。除了知识，他们也需要学习面对社会生活，而在校外解决自己的问题，就是一种锻炼。因此我认为教学生在校外解决问题，是高中教师最重要的能力。

Coco

我认为高中教师最重要的能力是要能给学生提供规划未来的建议，特别是针对15~18岁这个年龄段的学生。在这一阶段，学生开始思考自己的未来，尤其需要教师的指导。以我为例，我在高中时，就希望自己日后成为教师。我的老师给了我相关的建议和指导，如今我已经实现了我的教师梦。

### ■ My answer

　　教育有两种基本的方法：告诉学生该做什么和教他自己解决问题。我相信好的高中教师会使用后一种方法，这样学生就可以在学校环境之外吃得开。高中生即将成为成年人，他们需要为生活中的新挑战做好准备。教师可以通过教学生自己去解决问题，来帮助他们做好（这种）准备。诚然，给学生一张答案清单让他们记住并通过考试是件更容易的事，但这种方法在学校环境之外并不奏效。对于生活中的问题，没有人能给出简单的答案。学生们需要了解在特定情况下评估利弊的过程，以便在没有正确答案时（也能）做出决定。一个好教师不仅会解释问题的答案，还会展示得出最佳答案的推理过程。高中教师应该避免让学生只是背答案。学生需要学习解决问题的过程，这样他们才能为成年生活做好准备。

# Topic 4
## 培训重点教师 or 所有教师各自上网课

Section 1 of 1

Your professor is teaching a class on teachers' development. Write a post responding to the professor's question.

**In your response, you should do the following.**
- Express and support your personal opinion.
- Make a contribution to the discussion in your own words.

An effective response will contain at least 100 words.

Professor

The whole society puts more importance on teaching results nowadays. Improving teachers' teaching skills becomes a heated point now. For better education, the city wants to help teachers of its high school improve their teaching with two considered choices: choose a group of excellent teachers (These teachers will attend a class led by an expert for additional training in how to teach effectively, and they will then come back to their schools and provide that training for the other teachers in the school.); or provide additional training in teaching effectively for all high school teachers, using online materials that each teacher will study individually. Which one of these two plans would you support? Why?

00:09:59  Hide Timer

Benjamin

I believe that online training should be provided to all teachers, which will improve the quality of teachers' teaching the most. With the help of online materials, many teachers can freely choose the learning time and length, and grasp the learning rhythm, which is conducive to improving the teaching level. In addition, this method also realizes the fairness of teachers' self-improvement.

Caroline

In my opinion, small class training should be adopted, which is most conducive to the improvement of teachers' teaching level. Small class training can save manpower, teacher costs, and reduce the pressure on the government and schools. In addition, the small class also helps the trainer to help the teacher one-on-one, which is conducive to the improvement of the teacher's teaching level.

## 审题 & 构思

Professor 提出问题，询问考生，哪一种方式最能帮助教师，针对所有教师进行网上培训，还是小班集训？Benjamin 更希望给所有教师进行线上培训。Caroline 更接受小班集训。

## My answer

If my city wanted to help teachers improve their teaching ability, I would suggest that a few selected teachers from each school attend a special training course.[1] Of first concern is the budget for such a program.[2] Schools are invariably short of cash, so they need to devise a program that maximizes resources. If a few teachers are gone to a special workshop, the schools won't have to arrange substitutes for many teachers or overtime pay for lots of teachers to attend classes after regular working hours.[3] The selected teachers will also understand the materials better if they are present at a workshop with an expert.[4] They can ask questions for clarification, and the expert can monitor the group to ensure that everyone has mastered the concepts before moving on. A small workshop is most efficient for keeping everyone on target.[5] The plan will save money and train teachers well. What's more, the special class will allow there is always at least a teacher at the school trained and available to help others.[6]

(174 words)

[1] 主题句：作者认为少量教师参加培训有利于教师提升教学水平。

[2] 论据一：这种方式有利于节省学校支出。

[3] 论据展开：少量教师参加培训不会对学校的日常工作和开支造成重大影响。

[4] 论据二：这种培训方式有助于教师提升教学水平。

[5] 论据展开：小班培训有利于参与教师获得最大收益。

[6] 收束全篇，总结论点论据。

Topic 4　培训重点教师 or 所有教师各自上网课

## Words & Phrases

special training course 专修课　　　　　　clarification 阐明

budget 预算　　　　　　　　　　　　　　monitor 监控

substitute 替代品　　　　　　　　　　　　keep everyone on target 让每个人都达到目标

参考译文

Professor

如今，整个社会越来越重视教学效果，提高教师的教学技能成为当前的热点。为了更好地教育，该城市想帮助高中教师提高他们的教学水平，现有两个可以考虑的选择：选择一组优秀的教师；（这些教师将参加由专家牵头的课程，接受如何进行有效教学的额外培训，然后他们将回到自己的学校，为学校的其他教师提供培训。）或为所有高中教师提供有效教学的额外培训，提供在线材料，每位教师可以单独学习。你会支持哪一个计划？为什么？

Benjamin

我认为应该为所有教师提供网络培训，这样对教师教学质量的提升效果最好。借助网上资料，很多教师可以自由地选择学习时间和学习长度，把握学习节奏，这样有利于提升教学水平。此外，这种方式也实现了教师自我提升方面的公平性。

Caroline

我认为应该采用小班培训的方式，这样最有利于教师提升教学水平。小班培训的方式可以节省人力、师资成本，减轻对政府和学校的（财政）压力。此外，小班培训也有利于培训师一对一地帮助教师，这样有利于教师教学水平的进步。

## ■ My answer

如果我的城市想帮助教师提高他们的教学能力，我建议从每所学校挑选一些教师参加一个特殊的培训课程。首先要考虑的是这样一个项目的预算。学校总是缺少资金，所以他们需要设计一个最大化利用资源的项目。如果一些教师去参加一个特殊的培训，学校不必为许多教师安排代课教师或因为许多教师在正常工作时间之外上课而给他们支付加班费。在有专家在场的培训课上，被选中的教师能更好地理解培训材料。他们可以请专家及时解释问题，并且专家可以监督小组的学习进展，以确保每个人在继续学习之前都掌握了相关必要的概念。小组学习的办法最容易使每个学员达成自己的学习目标。该计划既省钱，又达到了好的培训效果，因为这样可以保证学校里至少会有一名教师接受培训，这名教师接受培训后还可以帮助到别的教师。

# TOEFL
## 生 活 类

# Topic 5
## 政府建设大型设施要求人们搬迁对不对?

Section 1 of 1

Your professor is teaching a class on government. Write a post responding to the professor's question.

**In your response, you should do the following.**
- Express and support your personal opinion.
- Make a contribution to the discussion in your own words.

An effective response will contain at least 100 words.

Professor

Sometimes, due to some large construction led by government, people need to move to another place. Before next class, I want you to consider the following question: Is it always right for governments to ask people to move their businesses and houses to provide space for the construction of large structures (new roads, new dams, etc.)? Why?

Topic 5　政府建设大型设施要求人们搬迁对不对？

00:09:59  Hide Timer

Karen

I think it's reasonable to ask people to move because of large construction. When the government is carrying out large-scale construction, it often gathers wisdom and argues repeatedly, so such construction often brings positive effects to people. In addition, residents who need to move will be compensated by the government for better working and living conditions.

Leo

I don't think the government should ask people to move due to large construction. People are often deeply attached to the place where they live and work, and forcing people to leave can be traumatizing. This is not only bad for personal development, but also causes hidden dangers to society.

| Cut | Paste | Undo | Redo | | Hide Word Count | 0 |

**审题 & 构思**

Professor 提出问题，人们是否应该为了政府的大型设施建设搬迁？

Karen 认为人们因为政府的大型设施建设而搬迁是合理的，因为这会对人们有利。如果以这里为突破点，完全可以再细化阐述，具体为搬迁为什么对个人会有利？比如可以举中国三峡大坝建设时，上游人们搬迁的例子。他们一部分人虽然离开了故土，迁往东部较远的地方，但也因此获得了在原地没有的工作机会，改善了个人甚至是一家子的生活水平。

Leo 认为强迫人们搬迁，对个人不好，也对社会不利。但这里没有详细展开，对个人哪里不好？对社会怎么不利？考生可以把这里当成突破点，组织语言进行扩展。

 **My answer**

Governments should never force people out of their homes and properties just to build dams, roads, or other large construction projects.[1] To start, governments usually claim that they pay for the land they take, so it is acceptable to force people to move. However, this superficial viewpoint does not accommodate for sites of emotional, spiritual, or historic value.[2] It is impossible for people to carry with them all the rocks, trees, or buildings that they grew up with. They may be offered money, but money cannot buy the emotional attachment that takes years—in some cases, generations—to develop. It is impossible to compensate for the irreplaceable objects linked to such memories.[3] Also, governments need to understand that forcing their citizens to comply is counterproductive because it destroys the governments' reputations.[4] People will become resentful and rebellious. For example, they may refuse to pay some taxes and stop participating in elections. They may be more inclined to break laws or ignore penalties as a sign of resistance. The entire political structure may become weakened if people are too upset about policies that were forced on them

**1** 主题句：政府不应该为了大型设施建设要求人们搬迁。

**2** 论点一：人们搬迁时无法带走原来居住地的历史文化物件。

**3** 论点展开：人们关于居住地的记忆，陪伴他们成长的一草一木无法用金钱补偿。

**4** 论点二：要求居民搬迁会损害政府声誉。

without their consent.5 For these reasons, governments should not make citizens move unless those people agree to do so. (205 words)

> [5] 论点展开，举例说明：人们一旦对政府产生不满，就会对本国的政治环境造成不良影响。

**Words & Phrases**

emotional attachment 情感依恋  　　resentful and rebellious 愤怒的和叛逆的
irreplaceable 不可替代的

Professor: 有时，由于政府主导了一些大型设施建设，人们需要搬到另一个地方。在下节课之前，我想让大家思考一下这个问题：政府要求人们搬迁他们的企业和房屋，为大型设施（新道路、新水坝等）的建设提供空间，这件事总是正确的吗？为什么？

Karen: 我认为，因为大型设施建设要求人们搬迁是合理的。政府在进行大型设施建设的时候，往往集思广益，反复论证，因此这类建设往往能给人们带来正面影响。此外，需要搬迁的居民会得到政府补偿，得到更好的工作、生活环境。

Leo: 我认为，政府不应该为了大型设施建设要求人们搬迁。人们对自己居住、工作的地方往往有很深的感情，如果强迫人们离开，那么可能会给他们带来精神创伤。这不仅不利于个人发展，也会对社会造成隐患。

### ■ My answer

　　政府不应该仅仅为了修建水坝、道路或其他大型建筑项目而强迫人们离开自己的家园和财产。首先，政府通常声称他们为他们征用的土地支付了费用，所以强迫人们搬迁是合理的。然而，这种肤浅的观点并不适用于具有情感、精神或历史价值的地方。人们不可能随身携带所有伴随他们长大的岩石、树木或建筑物。他们可能会得到金钱，但金钱买不到情感上的依恋，这种依恋需要几年的时间——在某些情况下，需要几代人的时间——才能形成。与这样的记忆联系在一起的不可替代的物品是无法补偿的。此外，政府需要明白，强迫公民遵守一些所谓的规定只会适得其反，因为这会破坏政府的声誉，人们会变得怨恨和叛逆。例如，他们可能会拒绝缴纳某些税款，并停止参加选举。他们可能更倾向于违法或无视惩罚，以此作为反抗的标志。如果人们对未经他们同意而强加给他们的政策过于不满，整个政治结构可能会被削弱。基于这些原因，政府不应该强迫公民搬迁，除非他们同意。

# Topic 6
# 改善健康靠控制饮食 or 适量锻炼 or 缓解压力?

Section 1 of 1

Your professor is teaching a class on health. Write a post responding to the professor's question.

**In your response, you should do the following.**
- Express and support your personal opinion.
- Make a contribution to the discussion in your own words.

An effective response will contain at least 100 words.

Professor

For this week's discussion, let's think about how to improve our health. Some people prefer to regulate their diet by carefully choosing kinds of food they eat. While others stress the importance of doing certain amount of exercise. Besides, relieving emotional stresses in our life may also affect the level of health standard. Which one of these ways do you prefer? Please use the discussion board to share your thoughts.

**Paul**

Doing a certain amount of exercise is one of the most active and effective means to build up the body. Physical exercise is beneficial to the growth of human bones and muscles, enhancing the function of heart and lung, improving the function of blood circulation system, respiratory system and digestive system. This is conducive to the growth and development of human body, improving the resistance to disease, and enhancing the adaptability of organisms.

**Emma**

I think we should improve our health by relieving stress. Nowadays people's pace of life is very fast, struggling with heavy work pressure and life pressure. According to the 2021 Emotional Health related survey, patients with depression accounted for 4.6% of the world population, so it can be seen that the impact of relieving emotional stress on physical health cannot be ignored.

### 审题 & 构思

本题是一道三选一的题目，教授讨论了如何改善健康的话题，给出了三种途径，分别是调节饮食、适量运动，以及缓解生活压力。

Paul 强调了适量运动的益处，比如可以提高身体各方面的机能，增强免疫力。如果你是一个酷爱健身的发烧友，沿着这个角度往下写应该不愁没有话说。可以结合自己健身的例子，描述一下健身给自己带来的积极变化。

Emma 给出了压力过大造成的弊端，比如患抑郁症的人的比例越来越高，来说明缓解压力对改善健康的重要性。如果你近来压力也不小，不妨用文字说说有效缓解压力对你来讲意味着什么。说考试的压力、生活的压力、社会的压力都行，但最终一定得写到这些压力怎么影响到你的健康指标。

### My answer

If I could only choose one thing to do to improve my health, I would regulate my diet better.[1] This is because my diet is a current weakness, but it is easy to regulate and to monitor progress.[2] I already exercise a fair amount, but can't resist a chocolate bar or carbonated drinks. I already know it is better to select, for example, a piece of fruit rather than a slice of cake.[3] If I actually decided to fix my diet, it would not be hard to make adjustments to my eating patterns. In fact, I would not even have to drastically change every meal in order to become more fit; I could make slight changes like having one cookie instead of three for a snack. Probably if I watched my food intake more, I could become more physically fit in only a short time.[4] Since my diet is a current weakness, it is the first thing I would like to remedy in an attempt to maintain a better lifestyle.[5] (170 words)

[1] 主题句：注意饮食从而改善健康。

[2] 解释主题句：选择改善饮食的原因是这方面目前是弱点，它容易调节，也容易监测进展。

[3] 段内递进1：进一步解释饮食方面存在的弱点是无法抗拒零食。

[4] 段内递进2：给出调节饮食的具体方法，比如每餐减少零食的摄入量，这样不用做出很难的改变就能在短时间内见效。

[5] 总结陈述。

Topic 6　改善健康靠控制饮食 or 适量锻炼 or 缓解压力？　　163

**Words & Phrases**

a current weakness 当前的弱点　　make slight changes 稍作改动

a fair amount 相当多　　food intake 食物摄入量

carbonated drinks 碳酸饮料　　remedy in an attempt to maintain a better lifestyle 为了保持更好的生活方式而采取的补救措施

### 参考译文

Professor

在本周的讨论中，让我们想想如何改善健康。有些人喜欢通过仔细选择他们吃的食物种类来调节饮食。而另一些人则强调做一定量运动的重要性。此外，缓解我们生活中的情绪压力也可能提升健康水平。这其中你倾向于哪一种办法？请使用讨论板分享你的想法。

Paul

做一定量的运动是增强体质最积极有效的手段之一。体育锻炼有利于人体骨骼、肌肉的生长，增强心肺功能，改善血液循环系统、呼吸系统、消化系统的机能状况。这有利于人体的生长发育，提高抗病能力，增强有机体的适应能力。

Emma

我认为我们应该通过缓解压力来改善健康。现在人们的生活节奏非常快，工作压力和生活压力都很大。2021年情绪健康相关调查显示，抑郁症患者在全球人口中的占比高达4.6%。由此可见，缓解情绪压力对身体健康的影响不容忽视。

### My answer

如果只能选择一件事来改善健康，我会选择更好地调节饮食。因为这是我目前的弱点，但它很容易调节和监测进展。我已经做了相当多的运动，但还是忍不住要吃巧克力棒或喝碳酸饮料。例如，我已经知道选择水果比吃蛋糕更好。如果我真的决定改变饮食，调整饮食模式并不难。事实上，我甚至不需要为了变得更健康而彻底改变每顿饭；我可以做一些小改变，比如零食吃一块饼干而不是三块。也许如果我更注意我的食物摄入量，我可以在很短的时间内变得更健康。由于我的饮食是目前的弱点，这是我想要纠正的第一件事，以此来保持更好的生活方式。

# Topic 7
## 学生交朋友最好的方式是什么？

Section 1 of 1

Your professor is teaching a class on social science. Write a post responding to the professor's question.

**In your response, you should do the following.**
- Express and support your personal opinion.
- Make a contribution to the discussion in your own words.

An effective response will contain at least 100 words.

Professor

We all need friends. Friends are people with whom we share happiness and who can help us. There are many ways to build friendships, such as joining a sports team, participating in community activities, or traveling. What is your favorite way to make new friends?

00:09:59  Hide Timer

Elena

One way to make new friends is to joining a sports team. In sports competition, not all people can win, participants from the same team working for a common goal will enjoy a kind of "psychological friendship" in the process of cooperation. Therefore, it is easier for them to build up real friendship, because working together ties them closer.

Bill

It's easier to make new friends while traveling. For example, many young people will choose to stay in youth hostels, which will hold various activities from time to time, so that people can make friends quickly. What's more, youth hostels contain multi-rooms, bunk beds, and it's great to talk about your trip together. It's easy to meet like-minded travelers here.

Cut  Paste  Undo  Redo                    Hide Word Count  0

**审题 & 构思**

本题是一道三选一的题目，教授讨论了结交新朋友的方式，包括加入运动队、参加社区活动或者旅行。

Elena 表示加入运动队容易结交新朋友，因为在体育活动中队友协同合作容易建立"心理友谊"，从而发展真正的友谊。如果你身处学校的任何体育社团，或其他 STEM、文艺社团等，这就是很好的切入点。

Bill 表示旅行途中更容易结交新朋友，例如，居住青年旅社、参加旅社活动、与同住的驴友畅聊人生，容易遇到志同道合的人。这个角度对大学生朋友来说更好写。或者高中生们可以写写自己 gap year（如果你真有的话）遇到的人、事、景，以论述这个交友的主题。

 **My answer**

I think the best way for a student to make new friends is to participate in community activities.[1] People who participate in community activities may be all different ages, but they have at least one overlapping interest. Interests alone do not make a friendship, though. People must have the opportunity to spend time together or otherwise remain in touch. Community activities include participants who are all local, so there is a chance for the student to meet the other people again.[2] For example, if they volunteer to do weeding in a park, they may have an interest in plants and being outside. To complete this project, participants are likely to talk with each other, encouraging conversations and helping each other to reach the goal. In this process, they will get to know each other and gain a feeling of belonging which is the seed that grows into a healthy friendship. Also because they live close, they can exchange contact information and plan to develop the relationship further.[3] (167 words)

[1] 主题句：参加社区活动是交新朋友最好的方式。

[2] 解释主题句：参加社区活动的人，不仅有共同的兴趣爱好，并且有机会保持联系，这两点是建立友谊的基础。

[3] 举例论证：作者给出了一个社区组织在公园里除草活动的例子，参与者对植物和户外活动感兴趣，在活动的过程中互相交谈，协同合作，通过这种方式认识对方，留下联系方式，从而建立友谊。

Topic 7　学生交朋友最好的方式是什么？

| Words & Phrases | |
|---|---|
| overlapping interest 相同的兴趣 | a feeling of belonging 归属感 |
| remain in touch 保持联系 | exchange contact information 交换联系信息 |

参考译文

Professor

我们都需要朋友。朋友是我们与之分享快乐的对象，也是可以帮助我们的人。建立友谊的方式有很多种，比如加入运动队、参加社区活动，或者旅行。你最喜欢通过哪种方式结交新的朋友？

Elena

结交新朋友的一个方法是参加运动队。在体育比赛中，不是所有的人都能赢，来自同一个团队的参与者为了一个共同的目标而努力，在合作的过程中会享受一种"心理友谊"。因此，他们更容易建立真正的友谊，因为协同合作把他们联系得更紧密。

Bill

旅行途中更容易结交新朋友。比如，很多年轻人会选择入住青年旅社，旅社会不定期举办各种活动，会让人迅速交到朋友。而且，青年旅社有多人间，上下铺的住宿形式，大家可以一起畅聊旅途趣闻，这是一件很棒的事。在这里很容易遇见志同道合的旅行者。

■ My answer

　　我认为学生结交新朋友的最好方法是参加社区活动。参加社区活动的人可能年龄不同，但他们至少有一个相同的兴趣。然而，兴趣本身并不能建立友谊。人们必须有机会花时间在一起或以其他方式保持联系。社区活动的参与者都是当地人，所以学生有机会再次见到其他人。例如，志愿参加去公园除草活动的人，他们可能对植物和户外活动会感兴趣。为了完成这个项目，参与者会相互交谈，鼓励彼此进行对话，相互帮助以达到目标。在这个过程中，他们会相互了解，获得归属感，这就为健康友谊的发展种下了种子。也因为他们住得很近，大家可以交换联系信息，计划进一步发展关系。

# Topic 8
## 没有理由不讲礼貌？

**Section 1 of 1**

Your professor is teaching a class on social science. Write a post responding to the professor's question.

**In your response, you should do the following.**
- Express and support your personal opinion.
- Make a contribution to the discussion in your own words.

An effective response will contain at least 100 words.

Professor

Over the next few weeks, we are going to discuss about some basic rules of interpersonal relationships. The first topic is about being polite. So here's a question for the class dicussion board: Do you agree that there is never a reason for people to be rude (impolite) to another person? Why?

00:09:59  Hide Timer

Lily

I don't think you need to be polite all the time. For example, when we are waiting in line to buy tickets while traveling, we often encounter people who jump the line. Even if we politely remind them, they will still insist on cutting in line. If we keep giving in, these people will be even more brazen. It is not necessary to be polite to those who do not obey the rules.

Bob

Being polite to others is conducive to maintaining good social relations. Polite words and behavior are symbols of a person's good character. We always meet problems or difficulties in our work and life. So, we need the help of colleagues, friends, and sometimes even strangers. If we don't respond politely or treat others with kindness, we will have conflicts with others, which is not conducive to maintaining good social relationships. In this way, we will give others the impression of bad character. When we ask for help, it's hard to find someone to help us.

## 审题 & 构思

这是一道是非类的题目，需要考生分析讲礼貌的利弊。

Lily 提出面对插队不听劝告的人，没有必要保持礼貌。生活中一定有一些事让你有些怨气、让你有效处理还得有礼貌，但有些场合这么做确实很难。那就写出你认为不需要讲礼貌的时间、地点、事件背景，有理有据地论述清楚。

Bob 提出讲礼貌的人更容易维持良好的人际关系，在真需要帮助时可以得到朋友、同事，甚至陌生人的支持。

## My answer

I agree that there is never a time for rudeness.[1] To begin, being polite makes the world more pleasant.[2] People are relaxed when others are nice and smile, as opposed to being tense and upset if others are rude. The overall effects of both rudeness and politeness are spirals: People tend to do more of the same and intensify the prevailing feeling. For example, if you smile at others, they will smile back. Therefore, the best reason to be polite is that it will encourage others to avoid negative behaviors of their own.[3] Plus, it is important to remember that being polite doesn't cost anything.[4] Being rude and being polite are both free, so you do not have to sacrifice anything to get one or the other. Since they cost the same, it makes sense to be polite and make people happy than be rude and make people upset.[5] As a result, there are no occasions when being rude is better than being polite.[6] (163 words)

[1] 主题句：没有理由不礼貌。

[2] 论点一：讲礼貌让世界更和谐，更快达成目标。

[3] 观点解析：人际交往是相互的，你礼貌别人同样报以礼貌。

[4] 论点二：讲礼貌没有成本。

[5] 观点解析：无论礼貌与否都没有成本，礼貌可以让人们相处起来更开心，何乐而不为。

[6] 总结句，重申观点。

### Words & Phrases

as opposed to 与之相反

spiral 螺旋形；螺旋式

negative behaviors 消极行为

Topic 8　没有理由不讲礼貌？

## 参考译文

Professor

在接下来的几周里，我们将讨论一些人际关系的基本规则。第一个话题是关于礼貌。那么，这有一个问题请大家在课堂讨论板上讨论：你是否同意"人们没有任何理由对另一个人无礼"？为什么？

Lily

我认为并不需要一直保持礼貌。比如，我们在旅行途中排队买票时，经常遇到插队的人。就算我们礼貌提醒，但是他们依然会坚持插队，如果我们一直忍让，这些人会更加肆无忌惮。对于不遵守规则的人，保持礼貌是没有必要的。

Bob

对别人有礼貌有助于保持良好的社会关系。礼貌的言语和行为是一个人良好品格的象征。我们在工作和生活中总会遇到问题或困难。所以，我们需要同事、朋友，有时甚至是陌生人的帮助。如果我们不礼貌地回应或善待他人，我们就会与他人发生冲突，这不利于维持良好的社会关系。这样，我们会给别人留下人品不好的印象。当我们寻求帮助时，很难找到帮助我们的人。

### ■ My answer

我认为永远不应该有粗鲁的时候。首先，讲礼貌使世界更显愉快。当别人表现友好并且微笑时，人们会感到放松；而当别人粗鲁时，人们会感到紧张和不安。粗鲁和礼貌的总体影响都是螺旋式上升的：人们倾向于给出同样的反馈，加强主导感觉。例如，如果你对别人微笑，他们也会对你微笑。因此，保持礼貌的最好理由是它会鼓励别人避免他们自己的消极行为。另外，需要铭记的一点是，礼貌并不需要付出任何代价。粗鲁和礼貌都是免费的，所以你不必为了其中一个而牺牲任何东西。因为它们的表面成本是一样的，所以因有礼貌而让人高兴比因粗鲁而让人沮丧更有意义。因此，在任何情况下，粗鲁都不比礼貌好。

# Topic 9
# 年轻人是否缺乏独立性?

**Section 1 of 1**

Your professor is teaching a class on humanity. Write a post responding to the professor's question.

**In your response, you should do the following.**

- Express and support your personal opinion.
- Make a contribution to the discussion in your own words.

An effective response will contain at least 100 words.

Professor

For today's discussion, let's think about the problem of young people's lacking of independence. Some people think that young people nowadays are more dependent on their parents. At the same time, others believe that they do not have this problem at all and even become more independent than before. What is your take?

Topic 9　年轻人是否缺乏独立性?

00:09:59　Hide Timer

Amy

I think young people lack independence nowadays. Even in their 20s, many college students still rely on their parents to take care of them. Many can't cook, can't do laundry and lack basic life skills. In the past, children took care of themselves from an early age and even helped their parents look after their siblings.

Yolanda

I don't agree with Amy. Now more and more young people do part-time jobs or start their own businesses while they are in school and don't depend on their parents financially, so they can live apart from their parents earlier. It has become a trend for young people to live alone, and young people without self-care ability are just the exception.

Cut　Paste　Undo　Redo　　　　　Hide Word Count　0

💡 **审题 & 构思**

这是一道对比类的题目，讨论年轻人是否缺乏独立性。这个话题因人而异，我们身边这两类人都不少吧？

Amy 提出年轻人缺乏独立性，需要父母照顾，没有基本的生活技能。如果从这个角度切入，就得深入分析一下，你认为为什么有的年轻人会是这样？什么社会背景、什么个人境遇造成他们会是这样？他们有办法破解这种生活局面吗？

Yolanda 反驳 Amy 的观点，年轻人独居已经成为潮流，依赖父母的只是个例。90后、00后选择这种生活方式的也不少，有利有弊。想从这里找突破口的考生，可以写写有什么利？又有哪些弊？

📝 **My answer**

　　Modern young people are more dependent on their parents than young people were in the past.[1] First, I attribute that change to longer life spans.[2] People tend to live longer now than they did in the past. Since parents generally can expect to raise their children for a longer period of time, they are less likely to encourage their children's independence at an early age. As a result, parents are more likely to do chores and let the kids "be kids" than to teach life skills such as cooking and cleaning. Modern young people are therefore less prepared for life on their own than young people from earlier generations.[3] Second, technology has increased connectivity.[4] Compare a girl who went out of town to college twenty years ago to one who is in school now. The modern girl can message her parents multiple times a day and may video chat every evening. By contrast, the girl from a previous generation could only call or visit rarely, as long-distance telephones were expensive. That old time girl needed to be resourceful and handle every aspect of her daily life without the help of her parents.[5] (192 words)

[1] 主题句：现代孩子更依赖父母。
[2] 论点一：现代人的寿命更长。
[3] 观点解析：因为现代人的寿命更长，父母陪伴孩子的时间更长，不愿让孩子过早独立。在父母包揽家务的情况下，孩子的生活技能发展得慢，更依赖父母。
[4] 论点二：科技让联系更方便。
[5] 对比论证：作者对比了现在的大学生和过去的大学生与父母联系的紧密程度。过去联系不便，离家上学以后只能自己处理问题，现在可以每天打视频电话，发信息。

Topic 9 年轻人是否缺乏独立性？

## Words & Phrases

| | |
|---|---|
| life spans 寿命 | video chat 视频聊天 |
| do chores 做家务 | resourceful 足智多谋的 |
| connectivity 连接（度）；联结（度） | |

### 参考译文

Professor

在今天的讨论中，让我们来思考一下年轻人缺乏独立性的问题。有些人认为现在的年轻人更依赖他们的父母。与此同时，其他人认为他们根本没有这个问题，甚至变得比以前更独立了。你怎么看？

Amy

我认为现在年轻人是缺乏独立性的。很多大学生即便到了 20 几岁，依然依赖父母的照顾。很多人不会做饭，不会洗衣服，缺乏基本的生活技能。而在过去，孩子们从很小的时候就开始自己照顾自己，甚至还帮助父母照看兄弟姐妹。

Yolanda

我不同意 Amy 的观点。现在有越来越多的年轻人在上学期间就做兼职，或者自主创业，经济上不依赖父母的支持，因此他们能够更早地和父母分开生活。年轻人独居已经成为一种潮流，没有自理能力的年轻人只是个例。

### ■ My answer

　　现在的年轻人比过去的年轻人更依赖父母。首先，我把这种变化归因于寿命的延长。现在人们往往比过去活得更长。由于父母可以抚养孩子更长的时间，他们不太可能在孩子很小的时候就鼓励他们独立。父母更有可能承担家务，让孩子"做孩子"，而不是教他们做饭和打扫等生活技能。因此，与前几代年轻人相比，现代的年轻人对独立生活的准备不充分。第二，科技增强了互联互通。比较一下 20 年前出城上大学的女孩和现在在校读书的女孩。现代女大学生可以一天给父母发好几条信息，每天晚上都可以视频聊天。相比之下，上一代的女大学生很少打电话或回家，因为长途电话费很贵。上一代的女孩需要随机应变，在没有父母帮助的情况下处理好日常生活的方方面面。

# Topic 10
## 父母要不要每周给孩子零花钱？

Section 1 of 1

Your professor is teaching a class on social science. Write a post responding to the professor's question.

In your response, you should do the following.
- Express and support your personal opinion.
- Make a contribution to the discussion in your own words.

An effective response will contain at least 100 words.

Professor

Parents give their children weekly money to buy whatever they want. Some people think this can cause bad habits and ideas about money in children. Others think the opposite. What's your opinion? Please use the discussion board to share your thoughts.

Topic 10 父母要不要每周给孩子零花钱?

00:09:59  Hide Timer

Ella

Giving children pocket money every week can help them develop financial awareness. Handling money is crucial to a person's growth and we will be dealing with money throughout our lives. As long as the amount of pocket money is controlled and conforms to the family's economic situation, it will not have a bad effect on children.

Steffen

I agree with Ella. Parents can guide their children if they are worried about their spending. For example, prepare a book for children to record their income and expenditure. Get them into the habit of keeping track of everyday purchases. At the same time, parents can analyze with their children whether the consumption in the account book is reasonable and help them develop good consumption habits.

| Cut | Paste | Undo | Redo | Hide Word Count 0 |

## 审题 & 构思

这是一道对比类的题目，分析给孩子零花钱的利弊。在当今社会的大背景下，如果孩子真是一分钱零花钱都没有，也不现实。但给太多也不行，孩子会觉得这钱来得太容易。写一个度，也是一种角度。

Ella 提出给零花钱，可以培养孩子的理财意识。

Steffen 同意 Ella 的观点，并且做了延伸，举例说明如何帮助孩子养成良好的消费习惯。

## My answer

While kids may learn a bit about making budgets if they have allowances, I think it is better when kids do not get one.[1] Allowances can lead to many problems such as arguments over what parents will pay for, what needs to be done by kids to receive the money, and how the money can be spent.[2] Kids may take the money for granted if it is just given to them, so parents often give money for doing chores. That causes additional problems, however. Kids may adopt an attitude of not wanting to do anything around the house unless they get paid for it, whereas parents may want them to do certain tasks for free.[3] For example, if a boy gets a dollar for sweeping the house once a week, he may not want to sweep until one of his friends comes for an overnight. The parents feel that the job should be done for free because it is the boy's friend who will come and stay, but the boy wants a dollar, his usual rate for the chore. An allowance can create a sense of entitlement like this.[4] (187 words)

[1] 主题句：不应该给孩子零花钱。

[2] 解释主题句：不给孩子零花钱的原因是"因何给""如何花"的问题会引起争论。

[3] 段内递进：进一步解释零花钱的发放方式会引起的问题，直接给孩子的话孩子会认为获得钱理所当然；让孩子做家务来获得钱，又可能导致孩子形成没有零花钱就不做家务的态度。

[4] 举例论证：作者给出了一个关于通过打扫房间获得零花钱的例子。孩子平时每周打扫房间会得到1美元，但是因为有朋友突然造访需增加一次打扫房间的工作，这时男孩应不应该获得零花钱会引发争论。

Topic 10　父母要不要每周给孩子零花钱？　　179

**Words & Phrases**

take...for granted 认为……理所当然
do chores 做家务
adopt an attitude of 采取一种……样的态度
sweep the house 打扫房子
entitlement（拥有某物或做某事的）权利

### 参考译文

Professor

父母每周给他们的孩子零花钱，让他们买他们想要的东西。一些人认为这会导致孩子们对金钱产生一些坏习惯和想法，其他人则持相反的看法。你怎么看？请使用讨论板分享你的想法。

Ella

每周给孩子零花钱，有助于培养孩子的理财意识。处理金钱对一个人的成长至关重要，终其一生我们都要和金钱打交道。只要控制好零花钱的金额，符合家庭的经济状况，就不会对孩子有不良影响。

Steffen

我同意 Ella 的观点。如果担心孩子会乱花钱，家长可以从旁指导。比如为孩子准备一个记录收支情况的账本。让孩子养成记录日常消费的习惯。同时，父母可以和孩子一起分析账本中的消费是否合理，帮助孩子养成良好的消费习惯。

### My answer

虽然如果孩子们有零花钱，他们可能会学到一些关于制订预算的知识，但我认为孩子们没有零花钱会更好。零花钱会导致许多问题，比如会导致争论，父母会因为什么给钱，孩子需要做什么来得到钱，以及如何花这些钱。如果只是给他们钱，孩子们可能会认为拿到钱是理所当然的，所以父母经常让孩子做家务来得到钱。然而，那带来了额外的问题。孩子们可能会持这样一种态度，除非他们得到报酬，否则他们不想做任何家务，而父母可能希望他们免费做一些家务。例如，如果一个男孩每周可以通过打扫一次房子得到一美元的报酬，那他可能直到他的某个朋友来过夜之前才会打扫。父母觉得这项工作应该是免费的，因为这是男孩的朋友来过夜；但男孩想要那一美元，因为这是他通常做家务的价格。给零花钱可能给孩子造成这样一种权利感。

# Topic 11
## 经济条件不同的人能不能做朋友?

**Section 1 of 1**

Your professor is teaching a class on social science. Write a post responding to the professor's question.

**In your response, you should do the following.**
- Express and support your personal opinion.
- Make a contribution to the discussion in your own words.

An effective response will contain at least 100 words.

Professor

In general, it is easier for people in the same economic class to become friends. Some people think that two people can be good friends even if one person has more money than the other. Others think it is difficult for people of different economic strengths to understand each other very well. What is your take?

00:09:59   Hide Timer

Amy

I don't think people with different economic abilities can be friends. Friends often go out to dinner or parties together and need to share expenses. People with different spending powers can hardly keep a long-term relationship. For example, if I have only $200 a month and my classmate wants to eat at a restaurant that costs $500 per person, I can't participate in his activities. It's hard for us to be friends.

Bill

I don't agree with Amy. There are many influencing factors for people to get along with each other, such as character and personality, education background, experience, etc. Economic condition is only one of them, but not the deciding factor. As long as two people have the same hobby, it is possible for them to become friends. For example, rich people and ordinary people may like the same writer, so they have a lot to talk about. Thus, they can also become friends.

| Cut | Paste | Undo | Redo | Hide Word Count 0 |

审题 & 构思

这是一道是非类的题目，讨论不同经济阶层的人能不能做朋友。

Amy 提出经济能力不同的人，消费能力差异大，很难成为朋友。其切入角度：想想你自己身边的朋友都是什么经济状况？是不是大多数还是和你处于同一阶层的？你可能都没有意识到，一些潜在的因素使你们渐渐地走在一起。

Bill 提出只要两个人有共同的爱好，就有成为朋友的可能。其切入角度：生活中这样的例子也不少，"三人行必有我师"嘛；单纯以金钱划分人群群体，也太显俗气。

 My answer

I don't think there is any problem with two people who have different amounts of money being friends.[1] I think people from different financial worlds can teach each other about different lifestyles.[2] I had a friend, Shelly, who was from a very wealthy family that lived on a huge farm. It was always interesting to visit her home because I was able to learn to ride a horse, even though my family was not rich enough to afford one. At first, I assumed the relationship was one-sided: I could not offer Shelly anything other than a visit to a regular suburban home. However, it turned out that she could not cook because her family had a maid. When Shelly came to my house, we made meals together with my mom. We both shared something that the other did not have. My friendship with Shelly is proof that people with different amounts of money can be friends. We learn about different lifestyles, appreciate our own way of doing things, and interact within the acceptable limits we have set.[3] (177 words)

[1] 主题句：经济基础不同的人可以做朋友。

[2] 解释主题句：经济基础不同的人可以教对方了解不同的生活方式。

[3] 举例论证：作者给出了自己和朋友 Shelly 的例子，Shelly 家境富有，作者通过和她交朋友，学习了骑马。作者家境一般，Shelly 家里有仆人，她没有做过饭，于是到作者家里体验了自己做饭的乐趣。虽然两个人经济条件迥异，但是她们都有彼此没有的人生体验可以借鉴，仍然能成为朋友。

Topic 11　经济条件不同的人能不能做朋友?

| Words & Phrases | |
|---|---|
| ride a horse 骑马 | a regular suburban home 普通的郊区住宅 |
| afford 负担得起 | maid 女佣 |
| one-sided 单方面的 | interact within the acceptable limits we have set 在我们设置的可接受的范围内进行交往 |

### 参考译文

Professor: 一般来说，处于同一经济阶层的人更容易成为朋友。有些人认为两个人可以成为好朋友，即使一个人比另一个人更有钱。另一些人则认为，不同经济实力的人很难很好地相互理解。你怎么看？

Amy: 我认为经济能力不同的人不能做朋友。朋友之间经常一起出去聚餐或者聚会，需要分担消费。消费能力不一样的人很难长期地交往下去。比如，我每月只有200美元零花钱，而我的同学想去人均消费500美元的餐厅吃饭，我就不能参与他的活动了。我们也很难成为朋友。

Bill: 我不同意Amy的观点。影响人与人之间相处的因素有很多，比如性格和人品、学历、经历等，经济条件只是其中之一，并不是决定因素。只要两个人有共同的爱好，就有成为朋友的可能。比如，有钱人和普通人都可能会喜欢同一个作家，因此有很多共同语言，他们也可以发展成朋友。

### ▶ My answer

　　我不认为两个经济程度不同的人做朋友会有什么问题。我认为经济实力不同的人可以相互教会对方自己的生活方式。我有一个朋友叫Shelly，她来自一个非常富有的家庭，住在一个大农场里。去她家总是很有趣，因为我能够学会骑马，而我的家庭并不富裕，承担不起这项活动。起初，我以为这种关系是一边倒的：除了让Shelly去郊区的一户普通人家看看，我什么也不能给她。然而，事实证明并非如此。她家有一个女佣，所以她不会做饭。当Shelly来我家的时候，我们可以和我妈妈一起体会做饭的乐趣。我们相互分享对方所没有的东西。我和Shelly的友谊证明了经济层次不同的人，互相之间也可以成为朋友。我们各自学习对方不同的生活方式，欣赏自己做事的方式，并可以在我们设定的可接受范围内积极互动。

# TOEFL
## 社会类

# Topic 12
## 有钱就应该做慈善？

Section 1 of 1

Your professor is teaching a class on charity. Write a post responding to the professor's question.

**In your response, you should do the following.**
- Express and support your personal opinion.
- Make a contribution to the discussion in your own words.

An effective response will contain at least 100 words.

Professor

People always believe that richer people should have more social duties compared to ordinary citizens. With the development of society, some people may change their minds. Do you agree that the more money people have, the more they should give away to charities. Why?

Topic 12　有钱就应该做慈善？

00:09:59　　Hide Timer

Abel

I think rich people should contribute more to charity. With the existing social condition and social resources, the rich people have the chance to earn enough money, so they should contribute to the society. In addition, with the help of charity, the society will be better developed and more conducive to the wealth accumulation of the rich.

Beata

I don't think rich people should make more charitable contributions because people are free to use their money. The rich have often worked hard to achieve their wealth. So they have no obligation to devote more money and time to charity.

| Cut | Paste | Undo | Redo | Hide Word Count 0 |

### 审题 & 构思

Professor 提出问题：拥有财富的人是否应该为慈善做出更多投入和贡献？

Abel 认为有钱人的财富取之于社会，应该回馈社会。得到发展的社会更有利于有钱人赚取财富。其可切入角度：事实上很多名人做慈善，无论是真心做慈善还是不得不去做慈善，他们总比普通人去做慈善显得更得体，更有经济基础。

Beata 则认为，有钱人的财富是通过努力得来的，他们有权随意支配财富。其可切入角度：有钱人确实应该承担更多社会责任，但不等于他们必须得捐出自己的一部分财富，被迫做慈善。

### My answer

People should be able to spend money in any way they choose. There is no reason that people who earn more money should donate any of it to charities.[1] It is important to remember that everyone can choose whatever job they want and earn the associated salary.[2] It may seem that high-paid doctors or lawyers are unfairly compensated, but they earn every penny of the money they get. They had to study hard in universities and pass competitive interviews to get accepted to jobs.[3] Not only do people have the right to pursue different jobs, but they also can decide how they spend their money.[4] Let's look at a simple example: Should people be told what brand of spaghetti they must buy? Should they be limited to at most three pairs of socks when they made such a purchase? Those questions may seem very ridiculous, but it is the same as saying that rich people have other obligations related to spending their own money.[5]

It may seem like a good idea to have people who earn more money give more to charities. However, I disagree. I feel that people who earn a lot of money have worked hard

**[1]** 主题句：作者认为，并非越有钱越应该做慈善。

**[2]** 论点一：人们可以选择自己想干的工作和想要的薪水。

**[3]** 观点展开：高收入人群是通过勤奋工作才获得了更多财富。

**[4]** 论点二：人们有自由决定如何使用自己金钱的权利。

**[5]** 举例论证：人们有权利自由支配自己的财产。

for it and should be allowed to decide how to spend it.6    6 收束全篇，总结论点，即并非越有钱越要做慈善。
(210 words)

### Words & Phrases

spaghetti 意大利细面条     obligation 责任，义务
ridiculous 荒谬的

## 参考译文

Professor

人们总是认为富人应该比普通公民承担更多的社会责任。随着社会的发展，有些人会有不同的想法。你是否同意人们越有钱，就越应该捐给慈善机构？为什么？

Abel

我认为富有的人应该为慈善做出更多贡献。凭借现有的社会环境和社会资源，富有的人才会有机会赚取足够的钱，因此他们应该回馈社会。此外，借助慈善事业，社会会得到更好的发展，更有利于富人积累财富。

Beata

我认为富有的人不应该被要求做出更多慈善方面的贡献，因为人们有自由支配自己财富的权利。富人往往是通过艰苦的努力才拥有的财富。因此，他们没有义务为慈善事业投入更多的金钱和时间。

### My answer

人们应该能够以他们选择的任何方式花钱。赚更多钱的人没有理由把钱捐给慈善机构。重要的是，每个人都可以选择他们想要的工作，并赚取相应的薪水。高薪的医生或律师看似得到了不公平的财富，但他们赚的每一分钱都是自己挣的。他们必须在大学里努力学习，通过竞争激烈的面试才能得到这份工作。人们不仅有权追求不同的工作，而且还可以决定如何花钱。让我们看一个简单的例子：人们应该被告知他们必须买什么牌子的意大利面吗？当他们购买袜子时，他们是否应该被限制一次只能购买三双以内的袜子？那些问题可能看起来很荒谬，但这和评论说有钱人在支配自己的花费时，还必须得承担其他义务的逻辑是一样的。

让赚更多钱的人把更多的钱捐给慈善机构似乎是个好主意。然而，我不认同。我觉得那些赚了很多钱的人是通过自己努力工作换来的，他们有权决定如何使用属于他们自己的财产。

# Topic 13
## 要不要为了保护环境减缓经济发展?

Section 1 of 1

Your professor is teaching a class on city development. Write a post responding to the professor's question.

**In your response, you should do the following.**
- Express and support your personal opinion.
- Make a contribution to the discussion in your own words.

An effective response will contain at least 100 words.

Professor

Governments have duties to solve many problems their citizens facing to. In the past, economic growth is an important goal for governments. Nowadays, governments have new challenges. Economic growth and environmental protection, which one weighs heavier in your mind? Why?

00:09:59  Hide Timer

Billy

I think it's very important to keep the economic growth. Unlike environmental problems, economic development is more urgent. Without stable economic development, people's living standards will hardly be improved. It is the government's duty to ensure people's basic livelihood and needs. That's why I think it's most important to maintain economic growth.

Carmen

In my opinion, environmental development is more important. Natural disasters are frequent, because of today's serious environmental problems. Natural disasters are likely to bring losses to people, so the government should give priority to dealing with environmental problems to prevent the loss of people's lives and property.

## 审题 & 构思

Professor 抛出问题：是否要因为环境保护延缓经济发展？

Billy 认为为了保证人民的生活，应该优先发展经济。其切入角度：很多第三世界国家的自然环境并不好，环境污染很厉害，他们不是不知道环境保护的重要性，而是当前经济发展的程度，还顾不上考虑环境问题。

Carmen 的观点是：应该优先保护环境，防止自然灾害。其切入角度：对很多发达国家来讲，环境保护的优先级肯定是高于经济发展的。但它们也都经历过经济发展的优先级高于环境保护的优先级的那个历史时代。

## My answer

Saving the environment is a lofty ideal, but not practical in modern society. Today governments should pay more attention to economic growth than to concerns about the environment.[1] The government's first responsibility is to take care of its citizens.[2] There are pressing basic needs such as providing adequate housing, good education, reasonable medical care, and the opportunity to pursue a decent career. In order to achieve these goals, a society must be economically productive.[3] The government should strive to reach this most essential of goals and provide everyone with their basic needs before turning its attention to other less pressing responsibilities. In doing so, the government may have to make some environmental sacrifices.[4] For example, some forests may be cleared to provide farmland so everyone has food to eat, and the wood used to build homes to shelter people. However, that does not mean that the environment is totally destroyed. Some parts are used, but animals and plants will eventually adapt to the new conditions.[5] I think the government's first responsibility is to its citizens, so it should pursue economic gains over environmental protection despite some sacrifices.[6] (186 words)

[1] 主题句：确立作者观点，不应为了保护环境延缓经济发展。

[2] 论点一：政府的首要任务就是照顾自己人民的现实利益。

[3] 论点展开：政府要保证人民的基本需求，而维持经济发展是保证需求的首要条件。

[4] 论点二：政府应该优先处理人民的基本需求，为此可以付出一些生态代价。

[5] 举例说明：阐释经济发展所要必须付出的生态代价，以及这些代价并不会摧毁生态环境。

[6] 强调观点，收束全篇。

Topic 13　要不要为了保护环境减缓经济发展？　　193

**Words & Phrases**

lofty ideal 崇高的理想　　　　　　　　strive to 争取，努力
pressing basic needs 迫切的基本需求　　adapt to 适应
decent career 体面的职业

参考译文

Professor　政府有责任解决公民面临的许多问题。在过去，经济增长是政府的重要目标。如今，政府面临着新的挑战。经济发展和环境保护，你认为哪一个更重要？为什么？

Billy　我认为维持经济的发展至关重要。不同于环境问题，经济发展更为急迫。如果没有经济的稳定发展，人民的生活水平也很难提升。而保证人民基本生活和需求，正是政府的职责。因此，我认为维持经济发展最重要。

Carmen　我认为，环境发展更为重要。因为如今环境问题相当严峻，自然灾害频发。而自然灾害很可能为人民带来损失，因此政府应该优先处理环境问题，防止人民的生命和财产遭受损失。

■ **My answer**

　　虽然拯救环境是一个崇高的理想，但在现代社会并不现实。今天，政府应该更多地关注经济增长，而不是环境问题。政府的首要责任是照顾好公民。有一些基本需求较为紧迫，如提供充足的住房、良好的教育、合理的医疗保健和追求体面职业的机会。为了实现这些目标，一个社会必须具有经济生产力。政府应该努力实现这一最基本的目标——满足每个人的基本需求，然后再把注意力转向其他不那么紧迫的责任。在这样做的过程中，政府可能不得不做出一些环境方面的牺牲。例如，一些森林可能会被砍伐，以提供农田，保证食物需求；而木材则用来建造房屋，为人们提供住所。然而，那并不意味着环境被完全破坏了。虽然（经济发展的过程中）环境有所改变，但是动物和植物最终会适应新的环境。我认为政府的首要责任是对其公民负责，因此政府应该优先追求经济利益，而不是先考虑环境保护，尽管这里面会有一些代价。

# Topic 14
## 新能源 or 传统能源，哪个更好？

Section 1 of 1

Your professor is teaching a class on energy usage. Write a post responding to the professor's question.

**In your response, you should do the following.**
- Express and support your personal opinion.
- Make a contribution to the discussion in your own words.

An effective response will contain at least 100 words.

Professor

Energy sources are vital for society's development. Some argue that we should use cleaner energy sources to protect the environment, while others believe traditional energy sources like coal and oil are better because they are less expensive. What is your opinion?

00:09:59　　Hide Timer

Carl

I think traditional sources are better than cleaner energy sources, because the price of traditional energy is low, which is conducive to the development of large-scale production. In addition, the technology for traditional energy is highly developed, and the use of traditional energy for production is profitable for improving production efficiency.

Brenda

I prefer to think that we should develop new energy, which is good for improving the environment. Faced with severe environmental problems, the government must take environmental factors into account when making decisions. In addition, as technology improves, energy conversion becomes more efficient and less costly. Then new energy will have more advantages.

| Cut | Paste | Undo | Redo | Hide Word Count 0 |

**审题 & 构思**

Professor 提出观点：是应该使用清洁能源，还是应该继续使用传统能源？切入角度：你家的车是油车还是新能源汽车？或者，你认为你所在的城市里，应该拥有更多的油车？还是应该拥有更多的新能源汽车？

Carl 认为，因为价格低廉，生产效率高，人们应该使用传统能源。切入角度：新能源汽车有各种好，但就是充电不那么方便。冬天使用更不方便，耗电很快，纬度越靠北的城市，越不方便使用。

Brenda 认为，为了保护环境，应该使用新能源。切入角度：出于环保、油价上涨等因素的考虑，新能源汽车使用越来越广泛，政府也出台了很多补贴。另外，也不一定非局限在汽车上面，太阳能、光伏产业、航天新能源，也是可以撰写的方向。但这对考生的要求较高，需要熟悉相关领域，知道具体细节怎么表达。

 **My answer**

I think we should turn to cleaner energy sources rather than continue to rely on traditional sources like coal and oil.¹ To begin, it is imperative to change energy sources soon to help alleviate the environmental problems caused by use of traditional energy sources.² These traditional fuels are harmful to extract because habitats are damaged. For example, undersea oil leakage destroys ocean habitats and drilling creates noise that harms communication among fish and whales. Furthermore, greenhouse gasses generated by these fuels are irrevocably changing our climate, causing global warming and an increase in natural disasters like typhoons.³ We need to put a brake on activities that contribute to such devastating environmental change.⁴ Critics might claim that it is better to stay with the cheap, current methods of producing energy. Their arguments pale against the uncalculated costs of repairing the environmental damage caused by such systems.⁵ Even if the environment is not included in the calculations, though, it makes sense that cleaner sources will become less expensive as they are developed.⁶ Therefore, price should not be a factor when considering the merits of cleaner energy sources.⁷

**1** 主题句：点明观点，表明作者支持更换新能源。

**2** 论点一：使用新能源有利于改善环境。

**3** 论点展开：传统化石能源会对自然环境造成多重危害。

**4** 收束论点一，强调新能源的重要性。

**5** 让步，分析反方的观点，并表明其不合理之处。

**6** 观点进一步展开：新能源会随着使用而价格降低。

**7** 收束让步观点，强调新能源的压倒性优势。

To sum up[8], clean energy is better for the environment and can become competitive in price. Therefore, we should switch to clean energy options. (209 words)

[8] 收束全篇，总结论据论点。

| Words & Phrases | |
|---|---|
| imperative 迫切的 | irrevocably 不可挽回地 |
| alleviate 减轻 | put a brake on 踩刹车；削弱 |
| extract 提取 | devastating 毁灭性的 |
| undersea oil leakage 海底石油泄漏 | pale 显得逊色 |
| drill 钻孔 | |

### 参考译文

Professor

能源对社会发展至关重要。一些人认为我们应该使用更清洁的能源来保护环境，而另一些人则认为像煤和石油这样的传统能源更好，因为它们更便宜。你的观点是什么？

Carl

我认为传统能源优于清洁能源，因为传统能源的价格低廉，这样有利于发展大规模的生产。此外，针对传统能源的技术极为发达，使用传统能源用于生产有利于提升生产效率。

Brenda

我更倾向于认为应该发展新能源，这样有利于改善环境。面对严峻的环境问题，政府在决策时必须要考虑到环境的因素。此外，随着技术的发展，能源转化效率注定会提高，（新能源的使用）成本也会随之降低。届时新能源会具有更多优势。

### ■ My answer

我认为我们应该转向更清洁的能源，而不是继续依赖煤炭和石油等传统能源。首先，必须尽快改变能源，以帮助减轻由使用传统能源造成的环境问题。这些传统燃料的开采会导致动物栖息地受到破坏，因此对环境是有害的。例如，海底石油泄漏破坏了海洋栖息地，钻井产生的噪声损害了鱼类和鲸鱼之间的交流。此外，这些燃料产生的温室气体正在不可逆转地改变我们的气候，导致全球变暖和台风等自然灾害的增加。我们需要制止导致这种破坏性环境变化的活动。批评人士可能会声称，最好还是继续使用目前廉价的能源生产方法。与修复这些系统造成的环境破坏的无法计算的成本相比，他们的论点显得苍白无力。即使计算中没有考虑环境因素，但随着清洁能源的开发，它们的成本也会降低，这是合理的。因此，在考虑清洁能源的优点时，价格不应成为一个因素。

总之，清洁能源对环境更有利，而且在价格上具有竞争力。因此，我们应该转向选择清洁能源。

# Topic 15
# 在市中心划定无车区

Section 1 of 1

Your professor is teaching a class on city planning. Write a post responding to the professor's question.

In your response, you should do the following.
- Express and support your personal opinion.
- Make a contribution to the discussion in your own words.

An effective response will contain at least 100 words.

Professor

According to needs of city development, the government would like to plan to have some certain places for citizens. The government now plans to establish some car-free zones in the center of the city. Some like this plan for they believe it can help eliminating traffic congestion, while others dislike it because they would not be able to reach places like stores and restaurants by car in a convenient way. What do you think of this plan and why?

00:09:59   Hide Timer

April

As a resident of a big city, I can't imagine a car-free zone. Cars as a means of transportation, are mainly in order to meet people's traffic requirements. Therefore, the car-free zone represents that the transportation in this area is not convenient compared to other places, which is bad for the life of local people.

Brad

As a father of a kid, I love this idea. In my case, my children sometimes like to play on the road, but it is not safe. If there is a car-free zone, then my children and other children will have more places to play, which is good for their growth.

| Cut | Paste | Undo | Redo | Hide Word Count 0 |

### 审题 & 构思

Professor 提出问题：你是否喜欢无车区这一提议？切入角度：国内貌似没有这种无车区，没有这种实景感悟，所以这道题不容易写。换个角度想，体育场馆、足球场，像这些地方，是不是在一定范围内划定为无车区会好一点？

April 表示考虑到生活便利，不能理解这个提议。

Brad 从孩子发展的角度，支持这个提议。

### My answer

I think our city would greatly benefit from a car-free zone downtown.¹ First, the town will be more beautiful because there will be trees, flowers, and grass rather than just paved roads.² People can look at birds playing in a fountain rather than staring at a wall of cars.³ Second, residents will be happier because they can relax and enjoy the space.⁴ They will have less stress from coping with endless traffic congestion. There will be less noise from cars and engines, so it will be pleasant to sit on the benches and talk together or eat lunch outside. Instead of having to travel to nature, people can just step outside their workplace to enjoy the fresh air and greenery.⁵ Third, the environment will be better off with a car-free zone because there is less traffic causing pollution, and less greenhouse gasses emitted during long traffic jams.⁶ Although the car-free zone parks are not the same as wilderness, they still can provide essential food, shelter, and water for species.⁷ A car-free zone is beautiful and helps the residents and environment. For these reasons, I feel that it would be wise for the city to create a car-free zone downtown.⁸ ( 199 words)

**1** 主题句：点明作者的观点，即无车区有利于城市建设。

**2** 论点一：无车区可以让城市更加美丽。

**3** 论点展开：市民可以欣赏更多美景。

**4** 论点二：市民可以拥有更多休闲空间。

**5** 论点展开：无车区让人们可以享受户外时光，有利于居民的生活。

**6** 论点三：无车区有利于生态环境。

**7** 论点展开：无车区可以为城市里的物种提供生活空间。

**8** 收束全篇，总结论据论点。

Topic 15　在市中心划定无车区

**Words & Phrases**

traffic congestion 交通堵塞　　　　　　greenery 青葱的草木，绿色植物

Professor

根据城市发展的需要，政府打算为市民规划一些特定的场所。政府现在计划在市中心建立一些无车区。一些人喜欢这个计划，因为他们认为这可以帮助消除交通拥挤；而另一些人不喜欢这个提案，因为他们不能方便地开车到达像商店和餐馆这样的地方。你觉得这个计划怎么样？为什么？

April

作为大城市的居民，我无法想象无车区的存在。车作为交通工具，主要是为了满足人们的交通代步需求。因此，无车区就代表着该地区交通相较于其他地方不太便利，这不利于当地人民的生活。

Brad

作为一个孩子的爸爸，我非常喜欢这个提议。以我为例，我的孩子有时候会喜欢在道路上玩耍，但这其实是不安全的。如果有无车区，那么我的孩子和其他的孩子都能有更多的地方玩耍，这样有利于他们的成长。

## ■ My answer

　　我认为我们的城市将从市中心的无车区中受益匪浅。首先，城镇将变得更加美丽，因为那里将有树木、鲜花和草地，而不仅仅是铺砌的道路。人们可以看到在喷泉里玩耍的鸟儿，而不是盯着一堵汽车墙。其次，居民会更快乐，因为他们可以放松和享受空间。他们将减少由应对无休止的交通拥堵带来的压力。有了无车区之后，区域里汽车和引擎的噪声会更小，于是人们坐在长椅上聊天或在外面吃午饭会变得很愉快。人们只需走出工作场所，就能享受新鲜空气和绿色植物，而不必去大自然旅行。第三，无车区的环境会更好，因为造成污染的车辆减少了，长时间交通堵塞时排放的温室气体也减少了。虽然无车区公园与荒野不同，但它们仍然可以为生物提供必要的食物、住所和水。无车区很漂亮，对居民和环境都大有益处。基于这些原因，我觉得在市中心建立一个无车区是明智的。

# Topic 16
## 谦虚 or 展示自我，哪个更重要？

Section 1 of 1

Your professor is teaching a class on personal development. Write a post responding to the professor's question.

**In your response, you should do the following.**
- Express and support your personal opinion.
- Make a contribution to the discussion in your own words.

An effective response will contain at least 100 words.

Professor

In modern society, humility as a virtue is re-considered by people. In the meantime, the importance of presenting oneself gets attention from people. There is a saying that it is important to make sure that others know about your strengths and accomplishments; if you are not so, you will be never successful in life. What is your remark on this issue?

Topic 16　谦虚 or 展示自我，哪个更重要？

00:09:59　　Hide Timer

Chris

I think it's hard for people to succeed if they don't let others know their strengths. If no one knows your strengths, it's hard for them to trust you and give you a chance. So if you don't let others know your strengths, it's hard to succeed in life.

Daisy

I think you have a chance to succeed without letting people know your strengths and your merits. In the process of letting others know themselves, people must reveal themselves. Inevitably, many shortcomings will be revealed, thus missing some potential opportunities. On the contrary, if you don't expose yourself too much, sometimes you will win people's favor and get ahead.

| Cut | Paste | Undo | Redo |

Hide Word Count　0

## 审题 & 构思

Professor 提出问题：让别人了解自己的长处是否是成功的重要因素。切入角度：快速检索自己大脑中，有谦逊品质能成功的人，和有张扬态度能成功的人，看哪一个更适合自己就题发挥。

Chris 认为如果不让他人了解自己的长处，人们就很难获得成功。

Daisy 认为即使不让别人知道你的长处，你也有机会成功。

## My answer

I agree with Chris's point and want to add more reasons and examples.[1] First of all, in school, letting teachers or professors know about our academic attainments could lead to our academic success.[2] Having a tight schedule, teachers usually do not have enough time to learn about every student. Therefore, it is important for students to let their teachers know about their academic strengths, in order to gain more opportunities.[3] For example, when having the opportunity to introduce their students to a variety of contacts at research institutions or other universities, professors tend to recommend those who they think are more excellent.[4] Therefore, letting professors know our advantages allows us to gain a competitive edge over other students at school.[5] In addition, in job-hunting market, it is important to let our potential employers have a basic understanding of our professional strengths, which can contribute to our career success.[6] Nowadays, humility is not the best way to help us successfully secure a job. In this sense, only when we show our strengths to interviewers can we secure a decent job.[7] In conclusion, from my perspective, letting important or influential people know about our strengths and accomplishments is essential for our success.[8] (200 words)

[1] 主题句：作者认为应展示才能和成就。

[2] 论点一：展示自我有利于学业上获得成功。

[3] 观点展开，让老师更了解自己才有可能获得更多机会。

[4] 举例说明，让教授更了解自己可能收获更多机会。

[5] 收束论点一，强调让教授了解自己能增加竞争力，获得更多机会。

[6] 论点二：展示才能在工作中也有作用。

[7] 论点展开：当今社会，只有让雇主了解自己，才有机会让自己获得好工作。

[8] 收束全篇，总结论点论据。

Topic 16 谦虚 or 展示自我，哪个更重要？

**Words & Phrases**

a tight schedule 紧凑的日程安排　　humility 谦虚

gain a competitive edge over other students 获得比其他学生更具竞争力的优势

### 参考译文

Professor

在现代社会，谦逊作为一种美德被人们重新思考。与此同时，展示自己的重要性也得到了人们的关注。有一种说法是，确保别人知道你的长处和成就是很重要的；如果你不这样做，你的一生将永远不会成功。你怎么看这一论述？

Chris

我认为如果不让他人了解自己的优点，那么一个人就很难获得成功。如果没有人知道你的优点，他们就很难信任你并给予你机会。因此，如果不让他人了解你的长处，你就很难在生活中获得成功。

Daisy

我认为即使不让人了解你的优点和长处，你也有机会成功。在让别人了解自己的过程中，人们必定要袒露自我。不可避免地，很多缺点也会显露出来，从而失去一些潜在的机会。相反，如果不过度暴露自我，有时候你反而会赢得人们的好感，从而获得成功。

### My answer

我同意 Chris 的说法，接下来再补充一些理由和例子。首先，在学校里，让老师或教授知道我们的学术成就，可以给我们带来学术上的成功。由于时间紧凑，老师通常没有足够的时间来了解每一个学生。因此，为了获得更多的机会，学生让老师了解他们的学术优势是很重要的。比如，当有机会将学生介绍给研究机构或其他大学的各种联系人时，教授倾向于推荐他们认为更优秀的人。因此，让教授知道我们的优势可以让我们在学校里获得比其他学生更大的竞争优势。此外，在找工作时，让我们潜在的雇主对我们的专业优势有一个基本的了解是很重要的，这有助于我们的职业成功。如今，谦逊并不是帮助我们成功找到工作的最佳方式。从这个意义上说，只有当我们向面试官展示我们的优势时，我们才能获得一份体面的工作。总之，在我看来，让重要或有影响力的人知道我们的优势和成就对我们的成功至关重要。

# Topic 17
## 谁最需要政府补贴?

Section 1 of 1

Your professor is teaching a class on social science. Write a post responding to the professor's question.

**In your response, you should do the following.**
- Express and support your personal opinion.
- Make a contribution to the discussion in your own words.

An effective response will contain at least 100 words.

Professor

It is common that the government would provide financial support to citizens in need. Which of the following people do you think need government financial support most? People over 70 years old, young families with children or people who lost their jobs? What is your preference on this? Why?

00:09:59   Hide Timer

May

I think people who are over seventy years old should get the financial support. Compared with the young, they have a lower labor force and less access to wealth. Even with pensions, many old people still suffer a sharp drop in income. In addition, the elderly have to spend more on medical care, so they need government's support the most.

Lorry

I think unemployed people need government assistance the most because they need financial support to get back on their feet. In the process of unemployment, people's standard of living will fall seriously. In addition, people may face emotional problems such as a loss of self-confidence. So the government's financial aid helps people get up as quickly as possible.

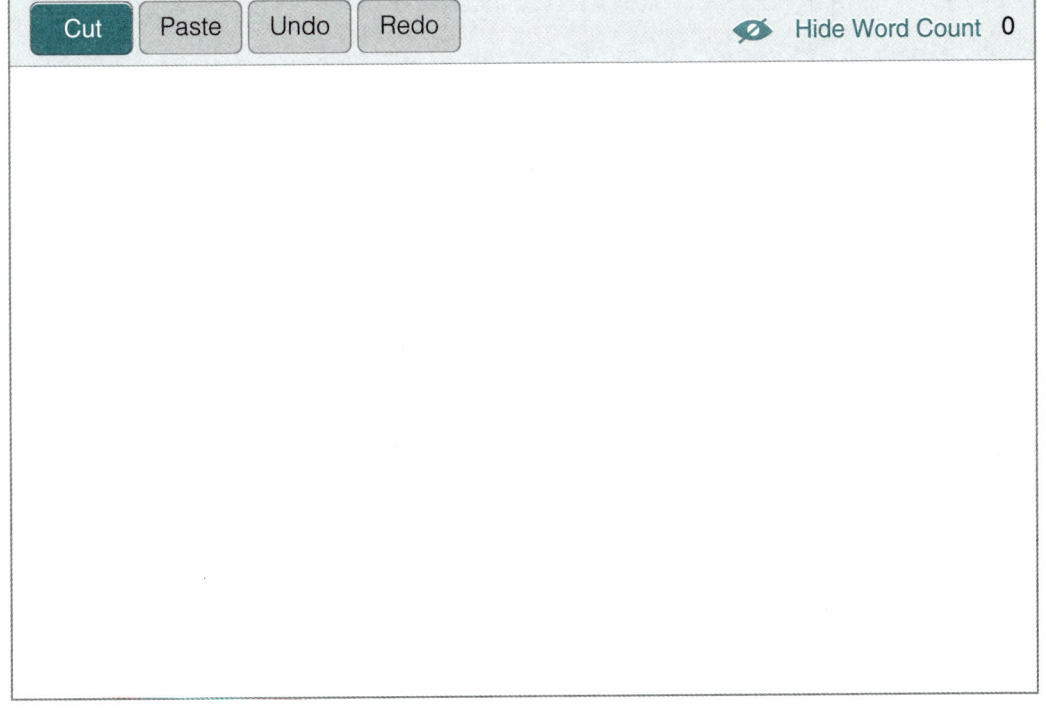

### 审题 & 构思

Professor 提出问题：政府最应该给哪一类人提供经济帮助？70 岁以上的老年人，有孩子的年轻家庭，还是失业者？切入角度：你是不是觉得这些人群都应该接受些补贴？那就太好了，说明你写哪个角度都会有内容可以发挥。

May 认为应该给 70 岁以上的老年人经济补助。Lorry 则认为应该给失业的人经济补助。

### My answer

As for the three choices given, I think young couples with children are more in need of financial support from the government.[1] For most young couples with children, one of the couple has to quit his/her job and stay at home to take care of their child wholeheartedly.[2] In this case, the quality of life of this family will sharply decline under the great pressure of life without government's financial support. That is because the family only has one person's income to cover all its expenses. Moreover, in today's society, raising a child definitely costs a lot. Even the most common daily necessities for children are also a huge cost for a family. Therefore, under such circumstances, it is a reasonable choice for the government to provide financial assistance to help those young couples, at least to help them through their children's infancy.[3] In conclusion, considering that young couples have their children to take care of and spend a lot on raising them, I firmly believe that these young couples are the most in need of financial support from the government.[4] (182 words)

[1] 主题句：表明作者立场，有孩子的年轻父母最应该得到补助。

[2] 观点展开，阐明现状：有孩子的年轻父母往往一方需要全职照顾子女。

[3] 观点展开：孩子花费巨大，因此，格外需要政府介入予以父母经济补助。

[4] 收束全篇，总结论据论点。

Topic 17　谁最需要政府补贴？

**Words & Phrases**

wholeheartedly 全心全意地　　financial assistance 经济补助
daily necessities 日常必需品

参考译文

Professor

政府向有需要的公民提供经济支持是很常见的。下列哪一类人群最需要政府的经济支持？70 岁以上的老年人？有孩子的年轻家庭？还是失业的人？你怎么认为？理由是什么？

May

我认为超过 70 岁的老年人最应该得到经济支持。相较于年轻人，他们的劳动力降低，不容易获得财富。即使有养老金，很多老年人的收入还是会明显下降。此外，老年人会在医疗上花费更多，因此他们最需要政府的补助。

Lorry

我认为失业的人最需要政府的补助，因为他们需要经济支持来重新振作。在失业的过程中，人们的生活水平会严重下降。此外，人们可能还要面对自信心受挫等情绪问题。因此，来自政府的经济补助，有利于帮助人们尽快振作。

### My answer

对于给出的三个选择，我认为有孩子的年轻夫妇更需要政府的经济支持。对于大多数有孩子的年轻夫妇来说，夫妻中的一方必须辞去工作，留在家里全心全意地照顾孩子。在这种情况下，在没有政府经济支持的巨大生活压力下，这个家庭的生活质量将急剧下降。那是因为这个家庭只有一个人的收入来支付所有的开支。此外，在当今社会，抚养一个孩子肯定要花很多钱。即使是最常见的孩子用的日用品，对一个家庭来说也是一笔巨大的开支。因此，在这种情况下，政府为那些年轻夫妇提供经济援助是一个合理的选择，这至少能帮助他们度过孩子的婴儿期。总之，考虑到年轻夫妇有他们的孩子要照顾，要花很多钱抚养孩子，我坚定地认为这些年轻夫妇最需要政府的经济支持。

# TOEFL

## 工作类

# Topic 18
# 想要商业成功必须打广告？

Section 1 of 1

Your professor is teaching a class on advertising. Write a post responding to the professor's question.

In your response, you should do the following.
- Express and support your personal opinion.
- Make a contribution to the discussion in your own words.

An effective response will contain at least 100 words.

Professor

We all know that business promotes its products through advertising. To create and distribute ads costs a lot. Before next class, I would like you to discuss on this statement: In order for any business to be successful, it must spend a lot of money on advertising. What do you think?

Topic 18　想要商业成功必须打广告？

00:09:59　　Hide Timer

Bill

I think it is necessary to spend a lot of money on advertising. For example, when I want to buy a new set of suits, the first thing I do is to search for related advertisements. By looking at ads and reviews, I can make a purchase in a convenient way. Without those ads, I have to wander from store to store, which is time-consuming and inefficiency.

Lucy

I don't agree with Bill. Advertising is necessary, but it doesn't have to cost a lot. Enterprises can promote their products by operating "self-media" accounts, which can achieve the effect of product promotion without investing a lot of money.

Cut　Paste　Undo　Redo　　　　　　　　　　Hide Word Count　0

### 审题 & 构思

这是一道是非类的题目，企业要想成功是不是必须花很多钱做广告？Professor 的切入角度：对又不对。生活中有的企业确实做了不少广告，正面、负面的效果都有。也有企业虽然没做广告，但却被它的客户在大众点评上推荐。

Bill 认可做广告的必要性，并给出了自己通过广告购买商品的例证。

Lucy 认为做广告不一定需要花很多钱。

### My answer

In order for a business to be successful, it must be willing to spend a lot of money on advertising.[1] It needs to reach a large enough audience to **build up a clientele**, to show that it has reputable products, and to offer reminders for people to return. A business needs to have a large number of customers to remain open, so it must advertise to attract customers.[2] It is important to remember that for every person who comes to the store, hundreds of others see the advertisement but do not enter. As a result, a business needs to pay for advertisements in a variety of places, or customers will never find it. Ads can vary from a large sign outside the business to television ads to print ads in magazines. A smaller business may consider paying someone to **hand out fliers**.[3] All of these methods of advertising, however, cost a significant amount of money if they are to reach a large number of **potential customers**.[4]

(166 words)

[1] 主题句：花大价钱做广告是有必要的。

[2] 解释主题句：商业成功需要建立顾客群，广告能让更多人了解公司的产品，产生潜在的顾客。

[3] 段内递进：进一步解释广告投放的地点和发放方式。

[4] 得出结论，重申观点。

**Words & Phrases**

build up a clientele 建立顾客群
hand out fliers 分发传单
potential customers 潜在的顾客

Topic 18　想要商业成功必须打广告？　215

### 参考译文

Professor

我们都知道企业通过广告推销产品。制作和分发广告的成本很高。在下节课之前，我想让你们讨论一下这个论述：任何企业要想成功，就必须在广告上花很多钱。关于这个问题，你怎么想？

Bill

我认为花很多钱做广告是必要的。例如，当我想买一套新的西装时，我做的第一件事就是搜索相关的广告。通过查看广告和评论，我可以方便地进行购买。没有那些广告，我不得不从一家商店逛到另一家商店，这既耗时又效率低下。

Lucy

我不同意 Bill 的观点。打广告是必要的，但是不一定需要花很多钱。企业可以通过经营自媒体账号来宣传产品，这种方式不需要投入大量的金钱，也能达到宣传产品的效果。

### ▎My answer

一个企业要想成功，就必须愿意在广告上多花钱。企业需要接触到足够多的受众，以建立客户群，展示自己有信誉良好的产品，并提醒人们回购。一个企业需要有大量的客户来保持营业，所以它必须做广告来吸引客户。重要的是要记住，对于每一个来到商店的人来说，成百上千的人看到了广告，但却没有进入。因此，企业需要在各种地方支付广告费用，否则客户将永远找不到它。广告的形式可以是企业外的大招牌、电视广告，再到杂志上的印刷广告。小型企业可能会考虑雇人发传单。然而，如果要接触到大量的潜在客户，所有这些广告方法都要花费大量的钱。

# Topic 19
## 不能接受批评的人在团队中是不会成功的

Section 1 of 1

Your professor is teaching a class on team working. Write a post responding to the professor's question.

**In your response, you should do the following.**
- Express and support your personal opinion.
- Make a contribution to the discussion in your own words.

An effective response will contain at least 100 words.

Professor

In teamwork, it is quite common for group members to have different opinions. Let's prepare our next class by discussing on this statement: People who cannot accept criticism will not succeed in working in teams. What do you think?

Topic 19　不能接受批评的人在团队中是不会成功的

00:09:59　　Hide Timer

Amy

People who work in teams must be able to accept criticism well. If they do not, there will be negative results in both the communication and the productivity of the team. If everyone works together and listens to advice, the end result is more effective.

Bob

I think accepting criticism benefits me in doing a group project. For example, last week, I represented my group to do a presentation. Other group members pointed out my habit of covering my mouth when talking, and I tried to fix it. As a result, I was able to pronounce my voice clearer than ever before and I got a lot of compliments. We got the best grade in class for our efforts, and that is due to the cooperation and willingness to accept criticism designed to improve our work.

Cut　Paste　Undo　Redo　　　　　　　　　Hide Word Count  0

 **审题 & 构思**

Professor 称不能接受批评的人在团队中是不会成功的。切入角度：忠言逆耳利于行。你曾身处的各种团队中，有没有人批评过你？你有没有批评过其他人？这些批评后来都怎么样了呢？产生了积极的还是消极的后果？

Amy 认为接受批评是必要的。

Bob 认为接受批评对团队合作是有好处的，给出了自己接受意见，并且获得成功的例子。

 **My answer**

Criticism is necessary for smooth social interactions in teams.[1] People who refuse to accept constructive advice about how to improve work or contribute fully will make the group members frustrated. If a person is not willing to make comments, the other group members will stop including that person in decisions. The person who does not accept criticism may then be viewed as acting superior or as draining group resources.[2] I remember working on a final project in a history class. All the students were allowed to pick groups of five, and my group included a friend who got angry if anyone criticized his work. We all ended up with a paper and building a model with very little input from that student, because he often walked out if we made suggestions about what he said. However, he ended up getting the same grade as we did, and we all were angry that he passed the class without offering help. Unfortunately, our friendship fell apart as a result of that experience, and we don't even talk to each other at all now. That would not have happened if he accepted criticism.[3] (189 words)

[1] 主题句：接受批评对团队活动顺利进行是必要的。

[2] 解释主题句：不接受批评的人显得傲慢，难以合作，会逐渐被团队孤立。

[3] 举例论证：作者给出了一个反面论据来佐证观点。历史课上做小组作业，其中一个组员不接受批评，小组活动参与度不高却获得了和大家相同的分数，引起了其他组员的不满，导致没有人愿意再与他合作了。

Topic 19　不能接受批评的人在团队中是不会成功的

**Words & Phrases**

smooth social interactions 顺畅的社交互动　　drain group resources 消耗团队资源
constructive advice 建设性意见

### 参考译文

Professor

在团队合作中，团队成员有不同的意见是很常见的。我们今天围绕下面这个陈述进行讨论，以更好地准备下节课的内容：不能接受批评的人在团队中是不会成功的。你怎么认为？

Amy

在团队中工作的人必须能够很好地接受批评。如果他们不这样做，就会对团队的沟通和生产力产生负面影响。如果每个人都一起工作，听取建议，最终的结果会更有效。

Bob

我认为接受批评对我做小组项目有好处。例如，上周，我代表我的小组做了一个报告。其他组员指出了我说话时捂嘴的习惯，我试着改正。结果，我能够比以前更清楚地发出我的声音，得到了很多赞美。由于我们的努力，我们在班上取得了最好的成绩，那都得益于我们愿意合作，并且愿意接受批评来改进我们的工作。

### ■ My answer

批评对团队活动顺利进行是必要的。拒绝接受建设性意见的人会使团队成员感到沮丧，比如关于如何改进工作的建议，以及如何充分为团队做出贡献的建议。如果一个人不愿意发表意见，其他小组成员就会不让那个人参与决策。不接受批评的人可能会被视为高人一等或消耗团队资源。我记得我在历史课上做一个期末项目，所有的学生都五人一组，我的小组里有一个朋友，如果有人批评他的作业，他就会生气。我们最后写了一篇论文，做了一个模型，但那个学生几乎没有怎么参与，因为如果我们对他说的话提出建议，他就会经常离开。但是，他最终得到了和我们一样的成绩，我们都很生气，因为他没有帮什么忙就通过了这门课。不幸的是，由于那次经历，我们的友谊破裂了，现在我们甚至都不怎么说话了。如果他接受批评，那样的事就不会发生。

# Topic 20
# 找工作的途径

Section 1 of 1

Your professor is teaching a class on career development. Write a post responding to the professor's question.

**In your response, you should do the following.**
- Express and support your personal opinion.
- Make a contribution to the discussion in your own words.

An effective response will contain at least 100 words.

Professor

For this week's discussion, let's think about ways of finding a job. Some people prefer to search for advertisements from companies through different medias such as newspapers. Others may ask friends for information on a job opening. Besides, sending letters to the company directly is also a possible way of getting a job. Which of these ways will you choose? Please use the discussion board to share your thoughts.

00:09:59   Hide Timer

Alice

I think the best way to find a job is by recommendation from friends. First of all, because our friends know our abilities and preferences, the job（s） they recommend would be highly suitable for us. Secondly, with the help of friends, we are more likely to get the chance of priority interview and have a higher probability of being hired.

Ben

I don't agree with Alice. The number of jobs friends can recommend is limited. In contrast, it is easier to find a job by searching job advertisements. Companies with recruitment needs will post information on the corresponding website. You can screen out many suitable positions at once, and you can communicate with the company's human resources in real time, which is very convenient.

| Cut | Paste | Undo | Redo | Hide Word Count | 0 |

**审题 & 构思**

本题是一道三选一题目，讨论找工作的方式。

Alice 表示通过朋友介绍更容易找到工作，朋友推荐的工作更适合我们。

Ben 不同意 Alice 的观点，因为朋友推荐的工作数量毕竟有限，通过搜索招聘广告更容易找工作。

 **My answer**

I think that the most successful way to find a good job is to send letters to the company I want to work for.[1] First, sending a letter proves that I am interested in the position.[2] It takes time and money to prepare and mail a complete introductory package. The hiring manager can see that I went to extra effort and will remember the presentation better than if he or she scans an electronic message.[3] Second, it also increases the chances of learning about jobs that are not advertised or job positions that hold to be released in the future.[4] For example, a person may have given notice about leaving, but the hiring manager has not yet posted the job on the Internet. Alternately, a department may be discussing adding new workers, but has not yet made the final decision to do so. My timely letter saves the hiring manager the effort of advertising the job because I have showed that I am available, qualified and interested.[5] By doing so, I show my interest, may find about jobs that are not advertised, and can be remembered for future positions.[6] (189 words)

[1] 主题句：写信申请是获得工作机会最好的方式。

[2] 论点一：写信表示我对工作职位感兴趣。

[3] 观点解析：写信详细介绍自己需要花额外的时间和金钱准备，给招聘经理留下更深刻的印象。

[4] 论点二：有机会了解尚未对外发布的职业空缺信息。

[5] 举例论证：比如一家公司有人即将离职，招聘经理正在考虑招聘，此时收到应聘者的信件，看到求职者不仅对工作感兴趣而且有任职资格，应聘者可能会直接获得工作机会。

[6] 总结陈述，重申观点。

## Words & Phrases

| | |
|---|---|
| introductory package 介绍性文件包 | have given notice about leaving 已经提出了离职 |
| hiring manager 人事部经理 | |

### 参考译文

Professor

在本周的讨论中，让我们想想找工作的方法。有些人喜欢通过报纸等不同的媒体搜索公司的广告，而其他人可能会向朋友询问职位空缺的信息。此外，直接给公司写信也是一种获得工作的可能方式。你会选择这些方式中的哪一种？请使用讨论板分享你的想法。

Alice

我认为找工作最好的方式是朋友介绍。首先，因为朋友了解我们的能力和喜好，所以他们推荐的工作会大概率适合我们。其次，有朋友帮忙，我们更容易获得优先面试的机会，入职的概率更大。

Ben

我不同意 Alice 的观点。朋友可以推荐的工作是有限的。相比之下，通过搜索招聘广告更容易找到工作。有招聘需求的公司，会在相应的网站上发布信息。你可以一次性筛选出很多适合的职位，并且能够和公司的人力资源进行实时沟通，非常方便。

### ■ My answer

我认为找到一份好工作最成功的方法是给我想要工作的公司写信。首先，写信证明我对这个职位感兴趣。准备和邮寄一个完整的介绍包需要时间和金钱。招聘经理可以看到我付出了额外的努力，而且比起浏览电子信息，他/她会更清楚地记住我的演示文稿。其次，它还增加了了解未发布或未来可能发布的工作机会的可能性。例如，（这个公司内部）一个人可能已经发出了离职通知，但招聘经理还没有在网上发布该空缺职位。另一种情况是，某个部门可能正在讨论增加新员工，但尚未做出最终决定。我及时的求职信省去了招聘经理发布广告进行招聘的麻烦，因为我已经证明了我是可以入职的、能胜任这个职位的，并且对这份工作是有兴趣的。通过这样做，我表明了我的兴趣，我可能会发现很多尚未对外发布广告的工作机会，并且未来有工作机会时，人力资源肯定会记得我。

# Topic 21
# 节假日不收发工作邮件能否提高员工的满意度？

Section 1 of 1

Your professor is teaching a class on business. Write a post responding to the professor's question.

**In your response, you should do the following.**
- Express and support your personal opinion.
- Make a contribution to the discussion in your own words.

An effective response will contain at least 100 words.

Professor

Some companies regulate that employees should not send or receive emails related to work on vacations or holidays. Some people believe that this policy would enhance employees' satisfaction. Others think the opposite. Do you think that it would be effective in enhancing employees' satisfaction? Why?

00:09:59  Hide Timer

David

The purpose of vacations is to relax and take one's mind off work. Such a break enhances work performance because the person is refreshed and able to look at the tasks with a new perspective. If the person deals with work-related emails during the vacation, the person would not get this needed refresh mind. Thinking about and doing a totally unrelated activity is essential to clear the exhausted mind. Such tasks as creative problem-solving or proofreading one's own documents are virtually impossible without a break that gives a new perspective. Therefore, it is a good policy to avoid work-related emails during vacations.

Smith

I agree with David. Dealing with work emails usually takes a long time. If you spend a lot of time on email during the holidays, you may feel like you're not really rested. It's more like working in a different place.

Cut  Paste  Undo  Redo                              Hide Word Count  0

**审题 & 构思**

这是一道是非类的题目，讨论节假日不收发与工作相关的邮件能否提高员工满意度。切入角度：这道题对诸多尚未走入工作岗位的考生来讲，不那么友好，毕竟还没工作呢，对自己假期需要收发邮件这件事，没那么感同身受。但如今大家基本都有 email 吧，校内作业布置也得用 email。大家可以想想，如果你在寒暑假中，还需要不得不收发来自老师的邮件，你会有什么情绪？把这个情绪迁移到你想象中未来的工作里，你就会有感而发。

David 认为休假是为了放松，从而使头脑更清醒。假期不应该处理与工作相关的电子邮件。

Smith 认为放假期间处理邮件像换了一个地方工作，没有得到真正的休息。

 **My answer**

Banning employees from sending work-related emails during vacations is a good policy that enhances employees' satisfaction.¹ If an employee must deal with work issues during vacations, that person might feel stress or resentment about the job. He may rush through the messages to complete them fast, or he may answer the messages while participating in other activities.² For example, they may try to answer emails on a smartphone while attending a baseball game, so they are not completely paying attention.³ Family members may also be frustrated and have arguments because the employee is busy with work rather than doing activities together. A resentful employee is not as productive as one who is happy. The stress from working during vacations could therefore interfere with effectively performing job duties. In extreme cases, it could lead to health issues caused by a lack of sleep, high blood pressure, or overeating due to stress.⁴ It is easy to avoid these problems by avoiding work emails during vacations.⁵ (163 words)

**1** 主题句：休假期间不收发工作邮件，肯定能提高员工的满意度。

**2** 解释主题句：休假期间处理邮件会让员工有压力，产生逆反心理，匆匆浏览，处理得不仔细。

**3** 举例论证：参加球赛时处理邮件无法集中精力。

**4** 段内递进：休假期间处理邮件会引发员工家属不满，进而让员工本人更为逆反，极端情况下引发身体健康问题。

**5** 总结句，重申观点。

Topic 21　节假日不收发工作邮件能否提高员工的满意度？

## Words & Phrases

work-related emails 与工作相关的邮件　　resentment 怨恨
enhance employees' satisfaction 提高员工满意度　　rush through 匆忙处理
deal with 处理　　productive 富有成效的

### 参考译文

Professor

有些公司规定，员工不应该在假期或节假日发送或接收与工作有关的电子邮件。一些人认为这项政策会提高员工的满意度，其他人则持相反的看法。你认为这会有效地提高员工的满意度吗？为什么？

David

度假的目的是放松，不去想工作。这样的休息可以提高工作表现，因为这个人会精神焕发，能够从一个新的角度看待任务。如果这个人在假期处理与工作有关的电子邮件，这个人就不会得到这种必要的精神休整。思考和做一件完全不相关的事情是清理疲倦头脑的必要条件。像创造性地解决问题或校对自己的文件这样的任务，如果没有休息，就几乎不可能有新的视角。因此，在度假期间避免收发与工作相关的电子邮件是个不错的策略。

Smith

我同意 David 的观点。处理工作邮件通常需要花费很长时间。放假期间，如果有很长时间花费在处理邮件上，那么你会觉得并没有得到真正的休息。更像是换了一个地方工作。

### ■ My answer

　　禁止员工在假期发送与工作相关的电子邮件是一项可以提高员工满意度的好政策。如果一个员工必须在假期处理工作问题，那么那个人可能会对工作感到有压力或怨恨。他可能会匆匆浏览信息以快速完成它们，或者他可能会在参加其他活动时回复信息。例如，他们可能会在参加棒球比赛时试图用智能手机回复电子邮件，所以他们没有完全集中注意力。家庭成员也可能因为这个员工忙于工作，不是一起参加活动而感到沮丧并发生争吵。一个心怀怨恨的员工不如一个快乐的员工工作效率高。因此，假期工作带来的压力可能会影响工作职责的有效履行。在极端情况下，它可能会导致睡眠不足、高血压或压力而致的暴饮暴食等引起的健康问题。如果在度假期间能够避免工作邮件的干扰，便很容易避免这些问题。

# Topic 22
## 好队友最重要的品质是什么？

**Section 1 of 1**

Your professor is teaching a class on teamworking. Write a post responding to the professor's question.

In your response, you should do the following.
- Express and support your personal opinion.
- Make a contribution to the discussion in your own words.

An effective response will contain at least 100 words.

Professor

Choosing the right teammates, whether in a school or a company setting, plays a significant role in the group's success. As a leader, which of the following do you think is the most important quality when choosing your teammates, honesty, the ability to get along well with others, or the ability to communicate clearly? I am more than happy to hear your points.

00:09:59  Hide Timer

Emma

I think honesty is a priority in picking teammates. Honesty is the foundation of building trust between people. Team members can only cooperate if they are honest with each other. I have complete confidence in the ability of my team members to complete the task, which is the most fundamental element of successful teamwork.

Lee

The ability to communicate clearly is the most important one among the three qualities mentioned by Professor. Everyone's perspective is different, and only by clearly expressing their own views can team members communicate effectively. It is difficult to collaborate with other members if you cannot clearly express your views, needs, or suggestions.

| Cut | Paste | Undo | Redo | Hide Word Count 0 |

**审题 & 构思**

这是一道三选一的题目，讨论选择队友时最看中的品质。切入角度：你处在什么团队中？团队中的这些人具备哪些品质？团队成员还具备哪些品质，可以使你这个团队变得更好？

Emma 认为诚实最重要，因为诚实是建立信任的基础。

Lee 认为清晰沟通的能力最重要，有效交流是成功的关键。

 **My answer**

I believe that the ability to get along with others is of paramount importance and thus my primary concern in choosing teammates.[1] Being able to relate well with others lays a solid foundation for excellent cooperation. When team members establish strong relationships with each other, they will let their guard down and then genuine communications set in, which facilitates active cooperation.[2] For example, once as a leader in a school assignment, I chose teammates who are very sociable and easy-going. We liked each other right off the bat, often hanging out together. In the group discussion, everyone took an active role in exchanging ideas, eager to contribute to the group. Had we not been able to get along well with each other, we would not have made such perfect teamwork. Then it dawned on me that the ability to foster a harmonious relationship is the prerequisite for any meaningful collaboration.[3] (151 words)

[1] 主题句：选队友时，与人相处的能力最重要。

[2] 解释主题句：能与人友好相处是团队成员建立关系，实现合作的基础。

[3] 举例论证：作者给出了自己做组长的经历，挑选好相处的组员，大家积极参与，共同合作，完美完成作业任务，佐证观点。

**Words & Phrases**

lay a solid foundation for 为……奠定坚实的基础　　right off the bat 马上，立刻

let their guard down 放下防备

## Topic 22 好队友最重要的品质是什么?

> **参考译文**

Professor

选择合适的队友,无论是在学校还是在公司,对团队的成功都起着重要的作用。作为一名领导者,在选择你的队友时,你认为以下哪一项是最重要的品质,诚实、与他人友好相处的能力,还是清晰沟通的能力?我非常乐意听听你们的看法。

Emma

我认为诚实是选择队友时要优先考虑的因素。诚实是人与人之间建立信任的基础。团队成员之间只有彼此坦诚相待,才能够实现合作。我完全相信我的队员能够完成任务,这是团队合作取得成功最基本的因素。

Lee

清晰沟通的能力是教授提到的三种品质中最重要的一种。每个人的视角都是不一样的,只有清晰地表达自己的观点,才能让团队成员有效交流。如果不能清晰地表达自己的观点、需求或建议,便很难和其他成员协同合作。

### ■ My answer

我认为与他人相处的能力是最重要的,因此这是我在选择队友时首先要考虑的因素。良好的人际关系为优秀的合作奠定了坚实的基础。当团队成员彼此之间建立起牢固的关系时,他们就会放下戒备,开始真正的交流,从而促进积极的合作。例如,在一次学校作业中,我作为组长,选择了非常善于交际和随和的队友。我们一开始就喜欢上了对方,经常一起出去玩。在小组讨论中,每个人都积极交流意见,渴望为小组做出贡献。如果我们不能很好地相处,我们就不会有如此完美的团队合作。然后我明白了,培养和谐关系的能力是任何有意义的合作的先决条件。

# TOEFL
## 政 府 类

# Topic 23
## 建新房 or 保护历史建筑?

**Section 1 of 1**

Your professor is teaching a class on architecture. Write a post responding to the professor's question.

**In your response, you should do the following.**
- Express and support your personal opinion.
- Make a contribution to the discussion in your own words.

An effective response will contain at least 100 words.

Professor

As witnesses of history, historical buildings have non-renewable characteristics. However, some argue that it's more important for the government to build new housing than to preserve old and historical buildings to meet people's needs for modern life. What's your take?

00:09:59  Hide Timer

Adam

Historic buildings are valuable cultural assets and can be maintained for generations. Critic may argue that it is too expensive to restore such an old building, but that is not necessarily true. Restoration ultimately saves natural resources because most of the materials are recycled as part of the new buildings.

Candy

I agree with Adam. In many cases, older buildings use materials that are no longer available at any cost, such as giant beams made from a single old tree. Original wood paneling, stone walls, and so on, can last for generations if properly maintained. By contrast, modern buildings made from compressed plywood and other cheap alternatives only last a few decades at most. In other words, it may cost less in the short run to erect a new building, but a historical building may require less money to maintain in the long run.

| Cut | Paste | Undo | Redo | Hide Word Count 0 |

### 审题 & 构思

这是一道二选一的题目，讨论政府应该保护古建筑还是应该建新房。切入角度：很多城市都面临这个问题，在新和旧之间选一个，在历史和现代中间选一个。但难道不能和谐共处吗？

Adam 认为，古建筑有不可替代的历史价值，修复并不会花费很多，因为有些材料可以重复利用。

Candy 同意 Adam 的观点，并进行了拓展，古建筑用的材料比新建筑更具有持久性，更有保护的价值。

### My answer

I think that when possible, it is better to try to preserve historic old buildings rather than tear them down to erect new housing.¹ Old buildings are a tangible reminder of the past that cannot be replaced. They are physical representations of the goals, aesthetics, and values of any given time period.² A good example is the manor houses in England, which many people say have outlived their usefulness and which should be torn down. A few summers ago, my family arranged to stay in a manor house that was turned into a hotel. I will never forget the experience: We slept in canopy beds draped in rich cloth and bathed in a big tub with clawed feet. The halls were made of dark wood and had old paintings. It felt like I had stepped back into the past. Later, I had to study about Victorian England in school. If I had not stayed in the manor house, I would not have appreciated the descriptions of the wealthy lords and the disparity between the upper and lower classes. Staying in the building provided a valuable lesson that could not be replaced with any video or lesson from a book.³ (199 words)

**1** 主题句：保护历史建筑更重要。

**2** 解释主题句：古建筑是历史的见证，展现了特定历史时期的特点。

**3** 举例论证：作者给出了自己参观古建筑的经历，置身其中的体验是任何视频或者书本给不了的，强调了保护历史建筑的作用。

Topic 23 建新房 or 保护历史建筑? 237

## Words & Phrases

| | |
|---|---|
| tangible reminder 有形的提醒 | canopy beds 带天篷的床 |
| physical representations 物理表征 | step back into the past 回到过去 |
| manor houses 庄园 | wealthy lords 富有的贵族 |
| outlive one's usefulness 失去效用 | disparity between the upper and lower classes 上层阶级和下层阶级之间的差距 |

### 参考译文

**Professor**

历史建筑作为历史的见证，具有不可更新的特点。然而，一些人认为政府更重要的工作是建造新的住房而不是保护古老的历史建筑来满足人们对现代生活的需求。你怎么看？

**Adam**

历史建筑是宝贵的文化资产，可以代代相传。批评家可能会说修复这样一座古建筑太贵了，但那未必是真的。修复最终节省了自然资源，因为大多数材料作为新建筑的一部分，可以被回收利用。

**Candy**

我同意 Adam 的观点。在许多情况下，古建筑使用的材料不惜一切代价也无法获得，比如由一棵老树制成的巨梁。原来的木镶板、石墙等，如果保养得当，可以代代相传。相比之下，由压缩胶合板和其他廉价替代品制成的现代建筑最多只能维持几十年。换句话说，建造一座新建筑可能在短期内花费更少，但从长远来看，维护一座历史建筑可能需要更少的钱。

### ■ My answer

我认为，在可能的情况下，最好是尽量保护历史悠久的老建筑，而不是把它们拆掉建新房子。古老的建筑是对过去的有形提醒，是无法取代的。它们是特定时期的目标、美学和价值观的物理表征。英国的庄园就是一个很好的例子，许多人说它们已经失去了使用价值，应该拆除。几年前的夏天，我的家人安排住在一个被改造成酒店的庄园里。我永远不会忘记那段经历：我们睡在盖着厚布的天篷床上，在一个有爪脚的大浴桶里洗澡。大厅是深色的木头，挂着古老的油画。感觉就像回到了过去。后来，我在学校学到了关于维多利亚时代的英国这一话题。如果我没有曾经住在庄园里，我就不会欣赏书中对豪门贵族的描写以及对上层阶级和下层阶级之间巨大差距的描述。待在那栋楼里的那段经历，给我上了宝贵的一课，这是任何视频或书本上的内容都无法取代的。

# Topic 24
## 为吸引游客，政府要不要改善治安和市貌？

Section 1 of 1

Your professor is teaching a class on tourism. Write a post responding to the professor's question.

**In your response, you should do the following.**
- Express and support your personal opinion.
- Make a contribution to the discussion in your own words.

An effective response will contain at least 100 words.

Professor

For this week's discussion, let's think about how to attract more tourists. Some people claim that the government should improve the safety by hiring more police. Others think that improving the appearance of the city is more effective. Before our next class, please use the discussion board to share your thoughts.

00:09:59  Hide Timer

Amy

If a city or country wants to attract more tourists, I think the best method is to improve its appearance. The purpose of travel is to relax. A place with beautiful scenery can bring people good mood. When choosing the tourist destination, the scenic place is more attractive, so I think the government should improve the appearance of the city.

Benjamin

I think to improve the city appearance is better than to hire more police. Hiring more police to improve security takes a lot of manpower and time, and the results are patchy. Improving the city is a one-off investment with obvious results. Beautiful scenery is more intuitive and more effective in attracting tourists.

| Cut | Paste | Undo | Redo | Hide Word Count 0 |

## 审题 & 构思

这是一道二选一的题目，讨论为了吸引游客，政府应该改善治安还是市容。切入角度：一城一策。想想那些治安很差的国家，你愿意去吗？想想那些很脏的地方，你有兴趣前往吗？这世界上治安好，环境又美的地方也不少，游客不请自来说明了什么？

Amy 认为，风景优美的地方能让游客放松，改善市貌使得城市更有吸引力。Benjamin 认为，改善市貌比雇用警察的效果更显而易见。

## My answer

I hold an opposite view as Amy and Benjamin do. Hiring more police is a clear solution to show that a country is invested in making a visit safe for tourists.[1] Safety is a primary concern when considering where to travel.[2] People do not want to go to a place that makes them worry about their personal safety or the safety of their possessions. That is especially true when parents are traveling with young children, or older people with less mobility. These types of people do not want excessive risks and breathtaking confrontations with disreputable thieves.[3] Police are on hand to stop crimes and solve problems that occur. Their very presence also prevents crime from happening.[4] Criminals will think twice, for example, about picking the pocket of a tourist when a police officer is standing nearby. Therefore, cities or countries should hire more officers to patrol the streets and investigate suspicious actions.[5] If a place has the reputation for being very strict about crime, people will be less likely to commit crimes, and the reputation for being a safe place will bring the place with more hidden benefits.[6] (188 words)

[1] 主题句：雇用更多警察，改善治安状况可以吸引更多游客。

[2] 段内递进1：安全是人们旅游要考虑的首要因素。

[3] 观点解析：出游时人们首先要保证人身安全，尤其是家里有老人和小孩时，不会去不安全的地方旅游。

[4] 段内递进2：警察能够预防罪犯犯罪。

[5] 举例论证：在街上有更多警察巡逻的时候，罪犯不容易作案。

[6] 总结句。

Topic 24　为吸引游客，政府要不要改善治安和市貌？

**Words & Phrases**

excessive risks 过度的风险
breathtaking confrontations 惊心动魄的对抗
disreputable thieves 臭名昭著的小偷
on hand 在近处

pick the pocket 偷钱包
patrol the streets and investigate suspicious actions 在街上巡逻，调查可疑行为
commit crimes 犯罪

## 参考译文

Professor

在本周的讨论中，让我们考虑一下如何吸引更多的游客。一些人认为政府应该雇用更多的警察来改善治安，其他人则认为改善城市的外观更有效。下次上课前，请在讨论区分享你的想法。

Amy

如果一个城市或国家想要吸引更多的游客，我认为最好的方法就是改善它的市容市貌。旅游的目的在于放松。风景优美的地方可以给人带来好心情。在选择旅游目的地时，风景优美的地方更吸引人，所以我认为政府应该改善城市面貌。

Benjamin

我认为改善城市面貌比雇用更多警察更好。雇用更多警察改善治安需要花费很多人力和时间，并且治安效果的改善并不稳定。改善城市面貌是一次性的投资，效果显而易见。优美的风景更加直观，对吸引游客更有效。

### ■ My answer

　　我和 Amy、Benjamin 的观点不同，雇用更多的警察是一个明确的解决方案，表明一个国家在为游客提供安全的旅行方面进行了投资。在考虑去哪里旅行时，安全是首要考虑的问题。人们肯定不想去一个让他们担心自己的人身安全或财产安全的地方。当父母带着年幼的孩子或者行动不便的老年人出行时，情况尤其如此。这类人不想冒太大的风险，也不想与声名狼藉的小偷发生惊险的冲突。警察可以随时随地制止犯罪，解决发生的问题。他们的存在也能预防犯罪的发生。例如，当警察站在附近时，犯罪分子想要扒窃游客的口袋时就会有所顾虑。因此，城市或国家应该雇用更多的警察巡逻街道，调查可疑行为。如果一个地方以严厉打击犯罪而闻名，人们就不太可能犯罪，安全的声誉将会给这个地方带来更多看不见的好处。

# Topic 25
## 投资实物 or 投资环境美化?

Section 1 of 1

Your professor is teaching a class on city development. Write a post responding to the professor's question.

**In your response, you should do the following.**
- Express and support your personal opinion.
- Make a contribution to the discussion in your own words.

An effective response will contain at least 100 words.

Professor

The government needs to be responsible for the urban construction. It is important for the government to provide money for things that are beautiful, not just for things that are practical. Before next class, I want you to consider if this statement is reasonable or not? Why?

00:09:59  Hide Timer

Mike

In my opinion, the government should invest in beautiful things, such as art galleries. Thus, it can cultivate the sentiment of citizens, so that people in the rapid development of the society could get a moment of peace. In addition, investment in art-related construction can also strengthen urban culture and civic pride.

Lily

In my opinion, the government should invest in practical things, because this kind of construction can quickly improve the quality of life of residents. Investing in stations, schools and hospitals can solve real problems in people's lives. Therefore, I think the government should invest in practical industries rather than beautiful ones.

| Cut | Paste | Undo | Redo | Hide Word Count  0 |

## 审题 & 构思

Professor 提出问题，政府应该将钱花在实际之处，还是花在能够美化城市的东西上？切入角度：哪个政府都面临这个价值判断问题，都在尽力找平衡。单独投入资金在哪一方面都会有问题。既然是讨论，完全可以选择"平衡"的观点。后文中，作者选择了站在"实用"的一边，因为这总比选择"美"的一边好写。

Mike 认为，政府应该把钱花在美的东西上，比如，举办艺术展。

Lily 认为，政府应该把钱花在实用的东西上。

## My answer

A government needs to focus on the basic needs of the citizens rather than spending superfluous money to beautify the city.[1] To begin, every government has a limited amount of money to divide among all the services it needs to provide.[2] If it spends money on artwork or flowers or other efforts to beautify the city, it will have less money to spend on essential services such as road repair, police and education. The government must set priorities, and unfortunately, that means that sometimes beauty must be sacrificed to meet those essential needs.[3] Furthermore, it must be noted that not everyone may like the artwork or other attempts to beautify the city.[4] How does the government decide which view of beauty is correct? Does the government have the right to determine what is appropriate for people of extremely diverse backgrounds to see in its public places? One person may feel a statue of a nude is beautiful, but another might find it an insult to religious beliefs. It is better for a city to avoid such conflicts.[5] Because it has limited budgets, the government should focus on practical expenditures rather than invest in unneeded attempts to beautify the city.[6] (199 words)

[1] 主题句：表明观点，即政府应投资实用类项目。

[2] 论点一：政府可支配的资源有限。

[3] 论点展开：政府需要对紧要的项目优先投资，对这些项目的投资优于投资艺术。

[4] 观点二：美很难定义。

[5] 观点展开：因为人对美的定义不同，政府很难建构符合所有人审美的事物，不同的审美可能会引发市民间的冲突，因此应该着力避免。

[6] 收束全篇：总结论点论据。

Topic 25　投资实物 or 投资环境美化？

**Words & Phrases**

superfluous 过剩的　　　　　　　　　　　nude 裸体的

essential needs 基本需求　　　　　　　　expenditure 花费，消费

参考译文

Professor

政府需要对城市建设负责，政府更应该为美丽的事物提供资金，而不仅仅是为实用的事物投资。在下节课之前，我想让你们思考一下这个观点是否合理？为什么？

Mike

我认为，政府应该投资美丽的事物，例如美术馆等。因为这能够陶冶市民的情操，让人们在高速发展的社会中获得片刻安宁。此外，投资艺术相关的建设，也能加强城市文化建设，增强市民自豪感。

Lily

我认为，政府应该投资实用类事物，因为这类建设能够较快提升居民的生活质量。投资车站、学校以及医院，都能解决人们生活中的实际问题。因此，我认为相较于美观的事物，政府应该投资实用的产业。

## My answer

　　政府应该关注市民的基本需求，而不是把多余的钱花在美化城市上。首先，每个政府都有有限的资金来分配给它需要提供的所有服务。如果它把钱花在艺术品、鲜花或其他美化城市的努力上，它花在道路维修、警察和教育等基本服务上的钱就会减少。政府必须确定要做的事情的优先级，不幸的是，那就意味着政府有时必须牺牲"美"来满足那些基本需求。此外，必须指出的是，并不是每个人都喜欢艺术作品或其他美化城市的尝试。政府如何决定哪种美的观点是正确的？政府是否有权决定背景极其多样化的人们在公共场所看什么是合适的？有人可能会觉得裸体雕像很美，但另一个人可能会觉得这是对宗教信仰的侮辱。对于一个城市来说，最好避免这样的冲突。由于预算有限，政府应该把重点放在实际支出上，而不是投资于不必要的美化城市的尝试。